CW00640953

Getting

from

Electronic
Meetings

Creative solutions

Increased commitment

Improved business processes

Alan Weatherall
Professor Jay Nunamaker

First published in Great Britain in 1999 by
Electronic Meeting Solutions Limited
23, Guildford Drive, Chandlers Ford
Hampshire SO53 3PS, UK

ISBN 0 9526525 1 X

Produced by St. Richard's Press Ltd
Leigh Road, Chichester, West Sussex PO19 2TU.

Introduction to the second edition

In the three years since the first edition of this book, the use of Electronic Meetings in all types of organizations and businesses has increased enormously.

The indications are clear that using computers to make meetings more effective will become a familiar feature of organizational life.

This second edition contains many new examples, including both face to face and 'distributed' meetings.

We hope that this book will help the reader achieve immediate benefits, and that it will remain a valuable source of ideas for the future.

German and Japanese translations are available of the first edition.

We wish you good fortune with the use of Electronic Meetings and would welcome your feedback.

Alan Weatherall
Jay Nunamaker
January 1999

The authors can be contacted by e-mail on:

aw@emsl.co.uk
nunamaker@bpa.arizona.edu

About the authors

Alan Weatherall

Alan Weatherall has worked for over 25 years at the leading edge of computer applications in business, much of this time with IBM, where in 1991 he first came across Electronic Meetings.

Since then he has planned, run and participated in hundreds of Electronic Meetings, and has designed and run many training courses on the subject.

With Jay Nunamaker and many others he shares a conviction that the use of computers to support meeting processes, teamwork and collaboration helps organizations become more creative and effective, and also enables individuals to make more of their skills and experience.

Jay Nunamaker

Jay Nunamaker is Regents and Soldwedel Professor of Management Information Systems, Computer Science and Communication at the University of Arizona. He is considered 'the father of Electronic Meetings' and is an internationally renowned authority on Groupware and computer supported decision-making. Among many honors for his work on Electronic Meetings, he was Andersen Consulting Professor of the year for 1992/3. In 1997 he was profiled by Forbes Magazine.

Jay is Chairman of Ventana Corporation, a spin-off company of the University of Arizona that develops and supports software for electronic interactions and decision support.

Acknowledgements

This book owes its existence to a lot of people.

Many people have worked on the development of Electronic Meetings. They have taken the technique from its first implementation with unwieldy technology to the present advanced use of networks around the world. These people had the faith and imagination to bring new ideas from early conception to the real world.

We acknowledge the following for their contributions to Electronic Meetings over the past fifteen years: Tony Adams, Betty Albert, Lynda Applegate, Mark Atkins, Mark Bovelsky, Janice Ceridwen, Minder Chen, Donald Coleman, Robert Daniels, Douglas Dean, Alan Dennis, Eileen Dennis, Gerardine DeSanctis, Gary Dickson, Joey George, Melissa Glynn, Ronald Grohowski, Glenda Hayes, Patricia Hollenbeck, Ann Hunt, Alan Heminger, Victor Kluck, Karen Knowles, Jeffrey Kottemann, Benn Konsynski, Helmut Krcmar, Frank Lancione, James Lee, Irene Liou, Donald Lynch, Amy McBride, Christopher McGoff, Scott McIntyre, William Ben Martz, Lynne Mikulich, John Milford, Daniel Mittleman, Gail Odom, Richard Orwig, Mark Prendergast, Brad Post, Bruce Reinig, John Richards, Nicholas Romano, Jeffery Sacks, Bill Saints, Lynne Schwarzmueller, Jack Stott, Bob Teo, Craig Tyran, Joseph Valacich, Douglas Vogel, Lee Walker, Kenneth Walsh, Ginny Wilkerson, Jerome Yen.

There is a larger group of people to whom acknowledgement is also due, but whom it is impossible to name individually. These are the people who are running Electronic Meetings in many different contexts in many different organizations around the world. Some of these people are mentioned in the text of the book.

For their help with the second edition of the book, the authors would like to thank Bob Briggs, Brian Helbrough, Jon Matthews, Peter Mullans, Brian Page and Neil Weatherall. We would like to thank Mila Denson of the US Naval Surface Warfare Center for providing one of the photographs on page 10. We would also like to express our grateful thanks to all the people who have made available to us examples of the successful use of Electronic Meetings, many of which we have not been able to include for reasons of space.

Most of all our thanks are due to our wives Coral and Nancy.

Comments on the first edition ...

This is a farsighted and unique guide to a technology that will in time benefit all businesses. Anyone involved in organizational processes should make it their business to read it.

Philip Jenks, *Business Age Magazine*

This book gives a taste of the opportunities and is written in a clear, logical and evangelistic style. This is an interesting book about an interesting new technique that should be read widely in the larger organization.

Peter J Pugh, *Professional Engineering Magazine*

Yes, it has finally arrived, the book on how to structure an Electronic Meeting. This book will tell you all you ever needed to know about how to make Electronic Meetings more effective.

Cosima Duggal, *Management Consultancy Magazine*

When I read this book, it really struck me that we should have started using Electronic Meetings two years ago.

Mary Jane Mitchell, *Director of Personnel*
Northumberland Community Health NHS Trust

The book describes a series of applications that showed the flexibility of Electronic Meetings and gave us a vision of the future as it could be. In the months after our first installation, our primary problem was managing the demand from people who wanted to use the tools.

Bob Dudley, *Internal Audit, National Grid*

An entertaining and informative read. I read it in one sitting and have effectively used my newfound knowledge ever since.

Nigel Dale, *Intranet Strategist, British Broadcasting Company*

Weatherall and Nunamaker illustrate with numerous cases how Electronic Meeting Systems can improve business processes in both the private and public sectors. Their book is the best example I've seen in specifically showing how businesses can increase performance with the use of technology.

Bruce Reinig, *Dept. of Information & Systems Management,*
Hong Kong University of Science & Technology

I think it is a fantastic book!

Mila Denson, *US Naval Surface Warfare Center*

This is the authoritative source of information about running Electronic Meetings, a comprehensive and rational book with real examples of cost benefits.

Carolyn Cukierman, *Battelle Institute*

... and on Electronic Meetings

I could deliver the message I wanted to the teams without resurrecting my "Atilla the Hun" image.

VP Fortune 500 Manufacturing Company

The Electronic Meeting Voting Tools permitted us to get past violent argument

Union Leader, *Transportation Industry*

Electronic Meetings have fundamentally altered the future of Naval Command and Control.

Captain Rick Williams, *Chief Architect of USS CORONADO*
Command Ship of the Future
Third Fleet and SPAWAR (Space and Naval Warfare)

Electronic Meetings increase the intellectual bandwidth of the interactions.

Former Executive Vice President, NCR Corporation

Using Electronic Meetings technology developed at the University of Arizona we reduced man-hours by 50% and project times by 90%.
Ron Grohowski, *former IBM Executive*

Electronic Meetings provide a forum for everyone to participate from "Gunner Boys" to "General Officers". The results are spectacular.
Don Lynch, *Former Brigadier General, Marine Corp*

With Electronic Meetings I can be directly involved with ten times the number of projects.
Partner, Big 4 Accounting Firm

Electronic Meetings is the enabling technology for a new type of organization - the virtual company.
Professor Lynda Applegate, *Harvard Business School.*

I have never seen so much thinking going on in a classroom in my life.
Judy Ayob, *Professor of Nursing, University of Arizona*

We work under extreme time pressure and every minute counts. Commenting and discussing an issue with everyone contributing in parallel leads to a wealth of information in a few minutes.
Scot Miller, *Commander, USS CORONADO, US Navy*

Our use of Electronic Meetings has significantly improved the productivity of workshops. Not only has the subject matter been explored in more depth, but each member of the workshop has been able to make a greater contribution.
Frank Hailstones, *Senior Partner, PricewaterhouseCoopers.*

Essentially, we work faster and smarter and get more done with less.
Shelley Walker, *Federal Aviation Administration.*

Two rooms set up for Electronic Meetings. Above, the U.S. Navy in an informal layout, below one of the permanent Electronic Meeting rooms at the University of Arizona.

CONTENTS

SETTING THE SCENE

Chapter 1

BETTER BUSINESS SOLUTIONS

This book describes exceptional developments in the use of computers to make meetings more effective. The objective of the book is to enable readers to benefit from such 'electronic' meetings.

Electronic Meetings are effective with as few as three participants and with over one hundred participants. Participants can be face to face in a meeting room or distributed around the globe.

People can use Electronic Meetings in their current responsibilities and expect to show immediate results. The techniques are well-established and ready to use. Introducing Electronic Meetings into an organization is low cost and low risk.

> You can expect to show immediate results.

This book will give examples of Electronic Meetings being used to develop solutions in every aspect of business, in government, in military establishments and in universities. Eight chapters are devoted to these examples.

A single Electronic Meeting can have a real impact on any project or team. Regular Electronic Meetings within projects or management processes can transform how people work together and how organizations operate. The intellectual capital of the entire organization can be tapped, including suppliers and customers when required.

Electronic Meetings can be run 'same time' or 'different time'. In 'different time' meetings the participants can join at whatever time during the meeting is convenient for them.

Meetings will always be an essential function in any project in any organization. In a good meeting the participants share knowledge and opinions, generate ideas for solutions, come to agreement and commit to action. The outcome of such meetings has a decisive influence on what the organization will try to achieve and how well it will perform.

Yet people from many organizations express the feeling that too many meetings are held, that time is wasted in meetings, that meetings take too long and that the right people do not attend. Projects and activities managed in these unsatisfactory meetings do not have the best chance of success.

The book describes how to improve this situation and develop solutions to make organizations more effective. It is based on practical techniques and real benefits achieved in all types of meetings and workshops in thousands of organizations.

> This book shows you how to develop solutions that make
> organizations more effective.

Electronic Meetings use a network of personal computers (PC's) to improve the communication that takes place in a meeting. The PC's are in use for typically 30 - 50% of the meeting. They do **not** eliminate conversation, discussion or humor from the meeting.

This book is not about the computing side of Electronic Meetings, so it does not require computer knowledge. If you can use a mouse then you have enough computing knowledge to use this book and to take advantage of Electronic Meetings.

> Participation is easy, is fun and does not require
> computer skills.

Electronic Meetings are a logical development of computing techniques. Just as it is now commonplace for people to have PC's on their desks, so large and medium sized organizations increasingly have networks of PC's capable of running Electronic Meetings. These PC's are often portable laptop computers so that Electronic Meetings can be held in any location.

> The computing technologies already exist and are proven.

The techniques for Electronic Meetings have been developed over the last 10 - 15 years, principally at the University of Arizona by teams working under the leadership of Professor Jay Nunamaker. Many of the applications discussed in this book are based on software called GroupSystems from Ventana Corporation, a spin-off company of the University of Arizona. There is now a wide range of software to help run Electronic Meetings, as can be seen in magazines and conferences, and by searching the World Wide Web.

It is useful in this context to distinguish between software that provides the infrastructure for Electronic Meetings and software that can actually run a meeting. Infrastructure software provides for example access to databases, network management, sharing of documents, private chat between participants, voice and video links and e-mail. Software that runs a meeting provides the functions of Electronic Meetings substantially as described in this book, including for example developing an agenda, and controlling activities such as discussions and votes.

The descriptions of Electronic Meetings in this book are at a general level, so as to be relatively independent of particular software.

As will be seen throughout the book, there are many benefits to be had from Electronic Meetings as a solution development tool. To get a feel of these benefits, you might like to ask yourself:

What would be the benefits to you if every meeting you attended ran in half the time?

This is a serious question, since studies have indicated a reduction of 50% or more in meeting duration, comparing Electronic Meetings with equivalent conventional meetings. And bear in mind that many managers spend between 40% and 70% of their time in meetings!

> The key people will attend, because meetings and workshops can be shorter.

But the measure of a successful meeting is not just to finish on time or even to finish early. A successful meeting must make its contribution to getting business results by exploring issues fully, creating better ideas, increasing commitment and starting effective actions. Electronic Meetings can be shown to do this.

A particular feature of Electronic Meetings is that participants' input can be anonymous. Although there are clearly many occasions in meetings when it is important to know who said what, anonymity in the right context is very powerful in helping to ensure that all the important questions, facts, theories, ideas, opinions and proposals are brought to the surface.

The technology of Electronic Meetings enables more people to participate than in conventional meetings, so that everyone with a relevant contribution can make their point and have it included. Since Electronic Meetings are more focused and shorter than equivalent conventional meetings, there is no bureaucratic overhead cost in these larger meetings.

A stunning innovation of Electronic Meetings is the ability to measure in detail the degree of consensus on a particular issue by using Electronic Voting. This quick and easy measurement significantly helps the meeting move to agreement and to action. It also reduces unnecessary discussion and saves time.

> Agreement and disagreement can actually be measured, thus focusing people on the important issues.

An Electronic Voting technique called 'matrix' voting allows participants to evaluate issues using multiple criteria (for example payback, profitability, effect on the environment, degree of risk, etc.). Matrix voting is described further in Chapter 13. It is an outstandingly better way to prioritize issues when the decision is important.

> Face to face meetings are becoming more important but less effective, as hierarchies become flatter.

Getting results from conventional meetings is becoming more difficult as organizations become flatter and as customers, suppliers and business partners expect to participate. For organizations facing the challenges of working in flat hierarchies with flexible, project-related teams, Electronic Meetings have arrived at just the right time.

Electronic Meetings encourage a more open organizational culture, based on the sentiments so frequently expressed in phrases such as 'involving everyone in the organization', 'teamwork is essential to our business', 'supplier partnerships' and 'we listen to our customers'.

Electronic Meetings provide an effective way to develop a *learning organization*, since the analysis behind decisions are automatically retained on computer, easily available for reference when comparable situations arise in the future.

But however wide the discussion, in most situations one person will still take the decisions. Electronic Meetings are perfectly effective if their objective is to help the decision-maker with ideas and opinions rather than to take the decisions.

> Electronic Meetings are effective whether one person or a team takes the decisions.

Participants in Electronic Meetings can be at different locations around the world and can participate in a meeting at different time. Hence travel costs are reduced, meetings can be held at very short notice and all the key people can attend.

> Participants can be in the same room or around the world.

Many organizations are already developing solutions using Electronic Meetings. **PricewaterhouseCoopers** found that Electronic Meetings "unlock innovation in an organization and drive it to action". **JP Morgan** have used Electronic Meetings to "enhance levels of innovation and creativity in an organization". The **US Army** has run successful Electronic Meetings with over 100 participants. **A hospital** in the United States has used Electronic Meetings to assess some of its suppliers. The **Amsterdam Municipal Police Force** has set up Electronic Meetings to develop systems to fight organized crime. **IBM** has run Product Satisfaction Workshops for their most dissatisfied customers using Electronic Meetings. **Boeing** have found that Electronic Meetings can reduce the elapsed time required for some projects by 90%. **Bellcore** saved $10,000 each time they ran a distributed Electronic Meeting. There are many other examples in this book.

Any individual manager of people or projects can take advantage of Electronic Meetings. Electronic Meetings are easy to set up. Skills are available around the world if the organization does not have them in-house. The computing equipment can be hired. Participants do not need training before the meeting, as tens of thousands of meetings have already shown. As more and more people in the organization use them successfully, Electronic Meetings will diffuse across the whole organization.

The people who benefit most from a new technique are those who move with it at the right time. The increasing use of networked PC's, both in the office and at home on the Internet, shows that people are now ready for Electronic Meetings.

> The time is NOW to use Electronic Meetings; this book will get you started.

From meetings to results

As has been discussed, meetings are an essential component of any significant organizational activity. A fundamental shift in how meetings are run transforms the ability of the people in an organization to develop new solutions for business problems and opportunities. Hence this book shows the way to improved business results, not just improved meetings.

How to use the book

Chapter 2 describes Electronic Meetings, what happens in them and why they are successful. The next eight chapters describe numerous examples of Electronic Meetings in real life for customers, in strategic planning, in business process re-engineering, supplier management and human resource management. Many of the examples give the name of a person or organization with a reference in the appendix.

Chapters 11 to 14 give more detail on the techniques of Electronic Meetings. Chapter 15 gives specific advice to meeting owners on how to get the most out of Electronic Meetings. Chapter 16 discusses the implementation of Electronic Meetings across the whole organization, which is a logical consequence of the wide range of applications that have been described in earlier chapters.

Finally Chapter 17 describes briefly how Electronic Meetings can be expected to become an essential daily tool in the organizations of the future.

The Appendix gives a checklist for running Electronic Meetings. The References section offers further information on many of the examples quoted in the text.

Chapter 2

OVERVIEW OF ELECTRONIC MEETINGS

This chapter describes how Electronic Meetings work and why they are effective.

What happens in Electronic Meetings?

Electronic Meetings are visibly different from conventional meetings in that participants use a Personal Computer (a PC) to record questions, opinions, ideas, facts, suggestions or votes.

One intangible difference from conventional meetings is that Electronic Meetings tend to have a very stimulating atmosphere. Participants know that they are likely to produce exceptional results with this powerful new tool.

The PC's are linked together on a network, either tabletop PC's or laptops.

The PC's are in use for typically 30 - 50% of the meeting. They assist in the communication process but do not dominate the meeting - there is still plenty of scope for discussion, conversation, banter and humor.

A large screen, such as one would expect to find in any conference room, displays the participants' input and other data as appropriate. A printer should be available with a photocopier in close proximity.

For some Electronic Meetings a facilitator may be present to help the chairperson run the meeting, for example large meetings or where the participants are new to the technology.

Many people are now familiar with the presence of a facilitator in meetings. A facilitator helps with the *planning and running* of the meeting but is not involved in the *content*. Hence, the facilitator would not input ideas and would not vote unless he or she was also a participant of the meeting.

During the meeting

The participants choose their seats and the chairperson opens the meeting. The objectives and agenda of the meeting are likely to be displayed electronically on the large screen and can also be available on the participants' PC's.

To start the meeting, participants may be asked to type some personal background information into their PC to explain what they bring to the party in terms of skills and experience. Participants can sometimes be surprised to learn something new and important about people they know well. This information can be immediately printed out, a much better arrangement than in a conventional meeting where one tries to take hurried notes as people introduce themselves verbally.

If participants are new to Electronic Meetings the next activity may be a fun electronic discussion of favorite holidays, sports, hobbies or some other diversionary subject. This would normally take no more than five minutes and helps to relax people who may be apprehensive about using computers.

An Electronic Meeting is a series of *sessions* or *activities*, each of which is started and stopped from one of the PC's on the network. During each session statements, questions or subject headings are sent to each PC via the network, asking for comments, answers or votes from the participants. For example:

- what worked well during this project?
- what should have been done differently?
- what ideas do you have to resolve this issue?
- what are the advantages of each of these proposals?
- what are the disadvantages of each of these proposals?
- what actions are needed?

The participants type their input into the PC, check it and send it across the network using the mouse or a function key. The input can now be available for all participants to see, usually anonymously so no one knows who made a particular comment.

Typing skills are not important. In fact the slow typist, by keeping input short in order to reduce the typing required, can communicate as effectively as the expert typist who enters long sentences at high speed.

Participants read all the input and add further comments as new thoughts are triggered. Thus the subject is quickly explored and recorded, to the extent required by the meeting owner.

The enthusiasm of the participants to communicate what they know and to give ideas sometimes results in a lot of input. The input can be reduced by *categorizing* or *merging* similar ideas, or by voting to select the most important.

At the end of the meeting, reports can be printed or transferred to e-mail for distribution. The whole content of the meeting, all the ideas and comments, are available if needed.

The meeting can be restarted at a later date if required, continuing exactly from the point it left off, with the same or with different participants.

Why Electronic Meetings are so effective

Electronic Meetings have many features that make them effective in driving towards solutions.

Clear structure

Electronic Meetings of necessity have a structure that is much clearer than that of a conventional meeting. The structure is contained in the agenda of the meeting, consisting of a series of sessions, one sequence of which is illustrated in Figure 2.1. These sessions are described in more detail in Chapters 11 - 14.

In Figure 2.1 the participants:

* talk about the subject, contributing facts and opinion - *exchange information and opinions.*
* input ideas or proposals as to what should be done - *develop proposals for action.*
* consider the pros and cons of the proposed actions - *evaluate ideas and solutions.*
* decide what should have priority and then agree who will do what - *vote on priorities and get commitment.*

Figure 2.1 - Typical sessions in an Electronic Meeting

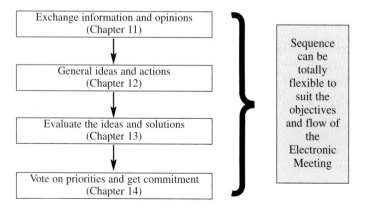

There are of course many different types of meeting and the sequence of an Electronic Meeting is completely flexible – and can easily be changed during the meeting.

The agenda should be prepared before the meeting, either specifically for that meeting or copied from a previous similar meeting. The agenda will often change during the meeting, for example to add sessions so that the participants can:

- exchange information and opinions on a new subject or a new angle that has spontaneously arisen in the meeting
- vote to focus a discussion
- liven up their creative juices with a suitable exercise.

Shared input

Comments, facts and opinions can be shared with all participants by being projected onto the large screen and/or displayed on each participant's PC. This helps avoid duplication of input and gives participants the opportunity to build on others' input, for example 'I agree/I don't agree with…'.

Parallel input

Participants type in their contributions at the same time, a much quicker process than waiting for each person to speak in turn.

Keyboard input

Recording one's contribution to a meeting via the keyboard allows participants to be sure that they have typed what they really mean before they send the input to other participants.

Anonymous input

As distinct from a conventional meeting, input in an Electronic Meeting can be anonymous. You may be outvoted later on your pet proposal, but at least you have a chance to tell the world about it - with the added benefit that no-one knows whether the idea came from the chairperson, the guru or the most junior person present. So each contribution is evaluated *on its own merits*.

This is a real benefit for everyone. Junior participants can make their contribution and even the most autocratic CEOs may wish from time to time to receive honest feedback. Research suggests that the best ideas do not come exclusively from senior management!

When input is anonymous participants are free to enter ideas or proposals that they have not yet fully thought out or that are based on uncertain information. In a conventional meeting it can be embarrassing if something you propose is less than ecstatically received, and this risk of embarrassment often smothers potentially valuable ideas. In an Electronic Meeting there is no loss of face if a half-baked idea is blown out of the water by other participants, because no-one need know who proposed the idea. Occasionally however, the half-baked idea is right on target, or is built upon by another participant with different knowledge and influence. Whoever proposed the idea can then modestly claim the credit! Hence the anonymity feature of Electronic Meetings enables better solutions to be defined than in conventional meetings.

It has been shown from experience that anonymity diffuses confrontation. Participants find it easier to respond to anonymous criticism than to the same criticism delivered eyeball to eyeball.

Of course there are many times when anonymity is not appropriate, when it is important to know who said what and whether an opinion is backed by knowledge and experience. The meeting owner can decide when anonymity is appropriate.

Participants are in any case quite free to include their name or title in any comment if they wish to emphasize their point, regardless of anonymity ('As VP of Quality my opinion is…').

Partial anonymity can be very powerful, whereby participants are identified by their department or function, but not individually. Thus we can see which comments are made by customers and which by marketing, but not the individuals who made them. This technique is illustrated in Chapter 12, Figure 12.4.

Electronic voting

Electronic Voting can be used to record formal decisions after a discussion, but it also has an important role in helping to focus discussion on the important issues. Before starting to discuss a subject, an Electronic Vote can establish what level of agreement there is between participants.

For example, if a quick Electronic Vote shows that the participants are split 50/50, then we know we probably need a longer discussion.

On the other hand, if an Electronic Vote shows 15:1 before discussion starts, then perhaps we don't need to spend too much time on the issue. It might still be important to know what is motivating the minority vote, maybe one individual has specialist knowledge or responsibility. But we do not have to waste valuable time while fifteen people talk through their common opinions before we realize that there is substantial agreement. Thus Electronic Voting saves considerable amounts of time in meetings.

Matrix Voting, or multiple criteria voting, opens up new horizons in group decision making. In Matrix Voting participants asses each issue against each criterion and the computer then does some simple arithmetic to summarize the votes. Participants can now see exactly where there is agreement and disagreement for each issue for each criterion, and focus the discussion accordingly. Typical criteria might be 'effect on the environment', 'speed of payback', 'growth rate', 'market chase', 'cost', 'degree of risk', etc.

Thus consensus can actually be measured in Electronic Meetings in ways which are quite impossible in conventional meetings. This is valuable in many situations, particularly in senior and cross-functional teams where it is important to have a common understanding of the degree of consensus, whoever actually takes the decisions.

Groups can work on different issues
In Electronic Meetings groups or individual participants can work on different issues in parallel and then share their results with the whole meeting. This is an effective way of ensuring best use of the participants' time and incidentally a powerful technique in situations of formal negotiation.

Other applications on the network
A logical consequence of using networked PC's in a meeting is that the PC's can access other systems for information that can contribute to the meeting, for example databases, spreadsheets, e-mail and the Internet.

Large meetings
It is often considered in a conventional meeting that about eight people is the maximum effective number of participants. This judgment can be rationalized by the calculation that eight participants can have a reasonable time to talk, seven and a half minutes per hour on average. But if one dominant character takes half the talk time...

In contrast, Electronic Meetings can be effective with 100 participants. This fundamentally changes how projects are planned and managed - we can now get all the people involved together, get their ideas, develop the plan and commit to it at one meeting. No hierarchies of meetings, with delays of days and weeks between them and endless confusion about what was actually said at each meeting.

Just for the record, small Electronic Meetings are effective with as few as four, three or even two participants.

Minutes of the meeting

In a conventional meeting it is generally impossible to take accurate notes of everything that has been said.

By contrast, in an Electronic Meeting all the facts, opinions, ideas and votes are stored on the computer. This record is immediately available. There is no delay and no dependency on hastily scrawled notes. The record can be printed, e-mailed or copied onto diskette, either the complete discussion or the conclusions. People who are not at the meeting can comment on it and learn from it. The record of the meeting can of course be deleted when that is appropriate

Such complete distribution of the actual content of a meeting is unique to Electronic Meetings and changes the perception of meetings. People no longer have to attend meetings simply to hear what is being said. Also participants are under a spotlight to do a thorough job because anyone with an interest can read the detailed report of the meeting.

A complete record of the meeting particularly helps people whose first language is not the language in which the meeting was held.

This instant availability of the complete record of Electronic Meetings will result in fewer meetings, decisions that are more informed and quicker implementation of actions, in other words better business solutions.

'Distributed' Electronic Meetings

To a world familiar with the Internet and the World Wide Web, it will be instantly clear that if the participants in an Electronic Meeting are using PC's on a network, they do not need to be in the same room or even on the same continent to receive other peoples' input and enter their own.

Distributed meetings can lack the personal touch of face to face meetings, and the remote participants may be adversely affected by less than perfect technology, for example, poor reception or slow response times. However, if there is serious business at stake and the alternatives are either inconvenient travel or unacceptable delay, then a distributed Electronic Meeting may be an excellent tool.

Distributed meetings are ideal to enable specialists in particular subjects to make their contribution to meetings without needing to travel or attend the whole meeting.

Experience has shown that high quality voice communication is desirable for distributed meetings. Electronic 'chat' facilities are also useful, whereby participants can send text messages to each other that are not part of the meeting, just as one might chat over coffee. Video-conferencing can be advantageous for this type of meeting, giving participants a greater feeling of personal contact.

For many aspects of a meeting, it may not be necessary that people participate at the same time. The meeting can be open for hours or even days while people join in from their offices or hotel rooms to make their comments and put in their proposals. This does not mean that participants have to spend hours or days in the meeting, but that they can contribute to the meeting at their own convenience.

Measuring success

This is another innovation of Electronic Meetings. Success can be measured at the end of the meeting by holding a short anonymous opinion survey to ask participants for their feedback. This is not to re-open the subject of the meeting, but to ask questions such as:

- did you find the meeting valuable?
- was the meeting well organized?
- did you feel able to contribute to the meeting?
- what was the best aspect of the meeting?
- what was the worst aspect of the meeting?
- what suggestions do you have for future actions?

The answers to these questions are shared instantly with the participants before the meeting closes.

The choice of questions for such surveys depends on the type of meeting, ranging from the 'tell' meetings, where the boss tells everyone what is going to happen, through to meetings of autonomous teams who make their own decisions.

There is an element of risk in asking such questions, since less than enthusiastic responses will require some positive leadership from the chairperson. However, an effective chairperson will use the responses to improve future meetings. The frequent result of this type of survey is to finish the meeting on a high.

What is wrong with conventional meetings?

This question has been answered at many Electronic Meetings. The reader might like to take a minute or two and jot down a few suggestions before reading the list below. Your list is likely include some of the following:

- the objectives of the meeting are not clear
- the right people do not attend the meeting
- the meeting is dominated by one person or group
- there is a reluctance to challenge
- people respond to the person rather than to what is said
- people do not listen all the time
- people talk in order to be seen to have said something
- the minutes of the meeting, if any, are issued late
- the minutes of the meeting are not accurate.

You may have added a few items to this list. By taking each of these bullets in turn and comparing them with the above list of features you can see that Electronic Meetings directly tackle all these problems.

Relating features to benefits

Hence Electronic Meetings show real benefits in relation to conventional meetings. These benefits include:

- meetings arranged earlier
- fewer meetings
- shorter meetings
- more/better ideas produced
- greater consensus and commitment
- immediate actions
- cash saving
- reduced time scales, i.e. projects completed earlier

Figure 2.2 relates these benefits to the principal features of Electronic Meetings as described above. Subsequent chapters of the book illustrate these benefits in more detail.

Figure 2.2 - Benefits of Electronic Meetings

Benefit	Feature
Fewer meetings	- feedback makes meetings more effective - electronic record
Shorter meetings	- clear structure of meeting - parallel input - shared input - Electronic Voting focuses discussion
Earlier meetings	- 'distributed' meetings
More/better ideas	- anonymity can help creativity - shared input avoids repetition - Electronic Voting - remote participants can put forward ideas
Greater commitment	- commitments are written down and very public - Electronic Voting - large meetings
Immediate actions	- meeting record available instantly - participants are committed
Cash saving	- 'different place' or 'distributed' meetings avoid travel - shorter meetings save time
Time scales reduced	- larger meetings get the whole team together - records of past meetings available

So let us look in the next eight chapters at how these features have been put to use in achieving business results.

GETTING RESULTS

Chapter 3

SATISFYING CUSTOMERS

Customers are becoming more demanding and it is increasingly difficult to provide competitive solutions that will give complete satisfaction. Many customers are indeed looking for solutions, not just for products or services. This means that organizations need better ways of identifying customers' requirements and responding to them. Electronic Meetings are ideal for these purposes, as this chapter will illustrate.

Focus groups

Traditionally a 'focus group' assembles a number of people together to ask for their opinions and requirements. A facilitator writes down or tape-records the input given by the participants. If each individual is to make a meaningful contribution, there may be a maximum of about ten participants at a traditional focus group.

Running a focus group as an Electronic Meeting has advantages that have been seen in Chapter 2. These include:

- opinions can be expressed freely since anonymity can be guaranteed
- requirements can easily be prioritized
- reasons behind requirements and opinions can be explored
- customer input is recorded directly and does not depend upon the judgment and endurance of the person who is taking notes
- more people can attend

- participants get immediate structured feedback that can be useful to them and hence encourage them to participate
- people can participate from different locations.

Laurene O'Donnell of Bellcore has used Electronic Meetings for focus groups with customers and employees. O'Donnell has found that numerous benefits can be realized, including saving time and reaching sensitive issues more quickly.

Linda Nicol of the IBM Canada Laboratory extended this approach by taking a network of laptop computers to business exhibitions in order to get customer input for future products. She found Electronic Meetings to be cheaper than conventional focus groups, measured in both absolute cost and cost per customer. Nicol has run Electronic Meeting focus groups on:

- market trends
- product requirements
- product prototype feedback
- partnership agreements.

As part of their input for product requirements, Nicol asked the customers to vote on the importance of different options, and to say how they would allocate money to these options. These two questions led to a detailed understanding of what the customers required. When collecting feedback on product prototypes, Nicol asked the customers to:

- identify the problems these products were intended to solve
- prioritize these problems
- say what they liked and disliked about the prototype and why
- summarize how competitive products compared
- estimate how much they would pay for the product.

The end result of each of these sessions is not a mass of data, but useful information, expressed in the customers' own words and already prioritized. A conventional focus group would not be able to obtain results at this level of detail and precision.

Evaluating customer satisfaction

Kathy Middendorf of IBM has used Electronic Meetings to help communication with customers by developing a one day Product Satisfaction Workshop. These workshops were for a selected set of customers - namely those who were the most dissatisfied. The formal objectives were:
- to understand the customers' concerns
- to increase customer satisfaction.

One question put to the customers went beyond the physical product to consider the total purchasing and ownership experience:

'What satisfies you about a software product? This includes your satisfaction with the software purchase, ownership, usage and service support.'

The customers were then asked to collectively prioritize their responses to this question. Subsequent questions asked the customers for any causes of dissatisfaction. The customers again prioritized their replies, and gave further, more detailed comments on the most important causes of dissatisfaction.

In a project to evaluate customer service delivery Carol Lindsay facilitated an Electronic Meeting for the Office of Personnel in Fairfax County, Virginia. Twenty six staff, about one third of the agency, developed lists of *things well done* and *areas for improvement*. The lists were then categorized by type of customer. Using the technology "jump-started the project by helping the agency to quickly generate a comprehensive list of ideas, eliminate duplicates and categorize them into manageable lists".

The telephone operators at KTAS, the Danish Telecom Company, were finding it a real challenge to decide which person or department they should connect external callers to as the product range became more complex and the company moved to become a solutions provider. The information psychologist and the head of staff set up an Electronic Meeting called 'The Right Connection, First Time'.

Some twenty employees representing different product and business areas participated in the Electronic Meeting. Initially they listed and commented on those situations that gave problems in connecting to the right person. This list of problems was edited, summarized and prioritized.

The participants then defined and agreed the causes of the prioritized problem areas. Finally the facilitator, Lars Ginnerup, introduced a 'what works well' session. This invited the participants to define the successful aspects of the present system that should be preserved, and also ensured that the workshop finished on a positive note. The whole meeting took only two and a half hours. It produced valuable proposals, some of which were implemented immediately.

Norwich Union uses Electronic Meeting facilities under the heading of a 'Collaborative Meeting Service'. A team from the Facilities Management Systems Department used the facility to develop ideas for improving satisfaction of their (internal) customers. Lead by Sue Cant, the Electronic Meeting included brainstorming and discussion sessions. It was completed in half a day, with participants "much impressed with how much we achieved in a very short time." "Above all, the session was fun!"

Care of the environment is an important issue these days for all customers. Nokia used Electronic Meetings in their Design for Environment process. Idea generating workshops were arranged for the product design experts to answer questions such as "How can you minimise energy consumption?". The designers were able to work independently to generate ideas and to comment on them at their own speed. In this way maximum use was made of the valuable time of the design experts. The ideas were rated and prioritized.

The first workshop generated 90 pages of ideas, votes and comments. The ideas were very well thought out and valuable also to other areas, not only environmental aspects. The results were used to form checklists for use in product proposals when deciding on Design for Environment strategies.

But if you really want to convince your customers that you care about their requirements, you use Electronic Meetings to let them help design your products.

Involving customers in product design

Consultant Lynn Daniel has used Electronic Meetings to involve customers in the design of both products and services. Daniel's experience is that customers can be a most valuable source of product design information and advice. Customers often like to participate in the design process, but there are some difficulties in their doing so using conventional techniques:

- customers may be unwilling to share sensitive information
- customers may not have thought through their future requirements
- customers may lack knowledge of possible future options
- customers are unwilling to give up time if there is no payback to themselves.

Electronic Meetings directly help overcome these problems. Anonymity solves the problem of sensitive information. The inter-activity enables customers to develop their picture of the future as they participate. The opportunity to exchange ideas with the other participants gives customers a real payback.

In addition to customers, a 'home team' from the marketing, design and manufacturing departments participates. The specific objectives of the meeting are to:

- summarize the problems or needs of the customer
- identify desirable features and benefits.

Daniel's first working session asks customers to input descriptions of their problems or needs, and prioritize them. Members of the 'home team' may answer or ask questions, but do not vote.

As a further measure of their priorities, Daniel asks the customers to allocate the design budget across their different proposals.

Where the information lacks detail or if there is disagreement between the customers about priorities, the issue can be explored in more depth. Thus the Design Department receives complete information at the end of the workshop. An area of disagreement between customers, if properly explored, can give useful information about possible market niches.

A final touch to Daniel's process is to run a subsequent Electronic Meeting internally, without the customers. Questions include 'what did the customers really say to us?', 'were there signals from the customers that we missed?' and of course an assessment of the value of the session.

Michael Boshes, a Human Factors Engineer with IBM Canada, has used Electronic Meetings to help develop new products by analyzing customers' jobs. A group of customers develops together a list of the tasks that they perform on their jobs. Participants then rate these tasks by importance and satisfaction. Tasks rated as of high importance but giving low satisfaction can represent possible opportunities for new products. More detail is then built up for selected tasks, including the goal of the task, the detailed steps from start to finish, the tools used and any bottlenecks.

"The results of the analysis consist of prioritized sets of tasks that represent the customers view of how they perform their jobs and how they would like future products and tools to support them." This information is invaluable for product designers.

In another example of identifying customer requirements, Paulette Buckingham of United States Transportation Command, with Larry Livernois of Coopers and Lybrand and Paul Frazier of Dynamics Research Corporation, worked with over 200 workshop attendees in groups of 15 - 25. They gathered input to determine which defense transportation systems should be regarded as 'best of breed'. Their summary included that the use of Electronic Meeting techniques:

".. was instrumental in being able to quantify individual and organizational positions. We were also able to keep volatile emotional factors at a manageable and tolerable level."

"This will benefit the warfighter by providing joint defense transportation systems… to improve the effectiveness and efficiency of the Defense Transportation System. The gain to the taxpayer is… monetary savings."

Emergency response

Perhaps the customers in the most urgent need are those who have just suffered disaster. The Federal Emergency Management Agency (FEMA) is an independent U.S. Government Agency whose role is to assist the American public in saving lives and protecting property from disasters and emergencies. Such projects frequently require involvement of staff from multiple locations and may require interaction with other organizations. Rick Neal and Martha Cole have described how FEMA uses distributed Electronic Meetings as a tool to help staff in different locations work together.

Summary:

The techniques of Electronic Meetings are revolutionizing the ways that organizations respond to their customers' requirements. Customers' opinions can be collated quickly, accurately, anonymously and cheaply.

Electronic Meetings can support Focus Groups and provide the basis for many types of customer workshops, including the involvement of customers in product and service design.

Gathering customers' requirements is part of a wider issue of defining a strategy for the organization. Strategic planning with Electronic Meetings is the subject of the next chapter.

Chapter 4

STRATEGIC PLANNING

Most organizations need a strategic plan. The strategic plan should include a vision of what the organization will look like in the future and a plan to make the transition. Strategic planning often includes the following activities:

* establish a vision and mission statement
* analyze the external environment
* analyze the internal organization
* develop different scenarios
* define objectives and goals
* define critical success factors
* define actions and measures.

The plan needs the commitment of the people who will carry it out. The different levels of the plan must be linked, from the broad strategy statements to specific actions. The plan will at times need quick revision, requiring that the process for strategic planning is straightforward and low cost.

Using Electronic Meetings the objectives of wide involvement, speed and reduced cost can be achieved. So let us see how this has been done.

Business strategic planning

The Royal Bank of Canada used an Electronic Meeting "to develop a strategy to regain a leadership position in Business

Banking". The conference, facilitated by Debbie Arsenault, of Deachman & Associates, was structured in line with the bank's four cornerstone objectives:

- customer satisfaction
- employee satisfaction
- portfolio quality
- business performance.

To ensure a proper focus on the customer satisfaction objectives, twenty Business Banking customers were invited to participate. The two hundred participants worked at individual tables of twenty people for some of the activities. For each objective the attendees discussed and prioritized best practices.

The over-all best strategies were presented in detail in plenary sessions. The input could be printed out to enable participants to pursue individual interests about particular strategies during the remainder of the conference. This was a quick and extremely effective process to share the most important strategies with the whole group. Arsenault reports that "the conference was a tremendous success with breakthrough strategies agreed to by all."

Facilitator Frank Bongers ran a set of strategic planning workshops for an agricultural organization in Holland using Electronic Meetings. The Dutch agricultural industry was facing large changes, including increasing international competition, new technologies and new environmental regulations. The organization wanted to use a participatory style of policy analysis, rather than an expert style, wherein a small number of experts develop the plans in isolation. Thirteen managers, employees and external stakeholders participated in a one-day workshop to develop and discuss in detail four scenarios. The scenarios included discussion of human resource issues, product-market combinations and strategic alliances.

A second one-day workshop with the same participants built upon these scenarios to explore the best and worst case outcomes, hence developing the most important options and choices for the organization. The project leader stated, "The scenario studies have accelerated, rationalized and opened the process".

In the detailed evaluation of this process, the participants rated the following propositions above four out of five on a five point scale (a GSS, a Group Support System, can in this context be taken to be an Electronic Meeting):

• GSS is a good tool to gain insight into the ideas of the group with regard to strategic options and choices
• The workshop increased my insight into possible relevant strategies for the organization.
• GSS is a good tool to increase the involvement of the participants with the strategy development of the organization.

Rosario Morales Campos and Ana Laura Torres Macias of the Center for Strategic Studies in Guadalajara have also used Electronic Meetings successfully in strategic planning. The objectives of their process include:

• identifying the vision, mission and strategic objectives for the company and its business units
• dynamically involving the participants in identifying specific objectives and projects.

There are four stages in this planning process:

• external and internal diagnosis
• strategic Business Unit identification
• specific objectives and projects identification
• project description.

For Stage I the participants need to be from the top of the company, with the authority to define the vision of the company for the next ten years. This stage also includes a SWOT analysis (Strengths, Weakness, Opportunities and Threats). In Stage II Strategic Business Units are discussed, based on issues of competition, customers, prices, quality and potential product substitution. In Stage III the participants (not the same senior people who lead stages I and II) develop specific objectives and projects for each Strategic Business Unit, down to the level of activities, dates and budgets for each project. Thus Electronic Meetings help define strategies, shape the organization and develop actions to achieve these strategies.

Ensuring that the strategy is effectively implemented is of course a major issue for strategic planners. Douglas Griffen has used Electronic Meetings to combine organizational strategy with leadership development. High performance teams are needed to achieve challenging objectives, and Griffen has used Electronic Meetings for:

- high performance team training
- individual skills assessment
- organization strategy initiatives.

The results of this approach, for one client at least, a KPMG State and Local Tax practice have been an exceptionally high level of growth.

In a summary of a number of strategic planning sessions carried out using Electronic Meetings Craig Tyran and colleagues have produced the analysis shown in Table 4.1.

Table 4.1 - Eight strategic planning meetings (Tyran)

Organization & tangible outputs	Group size	Duration of mtg.
ABC meeting 1 - prioritized list of company goals - list of SWOT issues ranked short and long term	31	2 days
ABC meeting 2 - strategies to promote competitive advantage - commitment to implement by specified date	27	1 day
ABC meeting 3 - proposals to improve linkages between departments - evaluation of current strategy	24	1 day
Gamma meeting 1 - list of opinions for corporate goals - evaluation of 17 divisional plans - list of short-term actions ranked by benefit, time sequence and feasibility	26	3 days
Gamma meeting 2 - list of opinions on competitive environment - resources needed from staff departments	22	2 days
Desert Utility - list of key organizational goals - list of strengths and weaknesses - list of key strategic issues, short and long term	30	2 days
Medical Center - list of key organizational goals	19	1 day
County Government - draft of county mission statement - prioritized list of key issues facing the county - strategies to address each of the top 5 issues	18	1 day

Tyran also measured what the participants thought about these meetings. The answers to his post session questionnaires are shown in Table 4.2.

Table 4.2 - Participants feedback on strategic planning meetings (Tyran)

Statement	% Agree	Neutral	Disagree
The computer-aided process is better than the manual one	85	10	5
I'm satisfied with the computer-aided process	81	11	8
I feel committed to the group's decisions	68	25	7
The computer-aided process helps: - generate ideas - identify key areas	 90 83	 5 12	 5 5

Thus 85% of the participants agreed that the Electronic Meetings process was better than the manual process. 90% of participants thought that Electronic Meetings help generate new ideas and over 80% declared themselves satisfied with the Electronic Meetings process. These are impressive results and establish that Electronic Meetings can be effective in strategic planning.

One particular figure in Table 4.2 raises some interesting thoughts. 68% of the participants felt committed to the group's decisions. This may not seem very high, but how do we compare this figure? One might think that such a basic question would be asked frequently at the end of meetings. However, the authors have seen no comparable figures where, after a conventional meeting, the participants have been asked if they feel committed to the results of the meeting, and have been given the opportunity to reply anonymously.

However, in Electronic Meetings you can ask this question and instantly show the answer to all the participants. If the percentage committed is too low, Electronic Meetings provide the mechanism to find out what the problem is, and then to tackle it. This is immensely powerful and impossible in conventional meetings. After all, how meaningful is a strategic planning meeting if at the end the participants do not feel committed to the meeting's decisions or recommendations?

Strategic planning in local Government

Carol Lindsay has described the use of an Electronic Meeting to develop an economic strategic plan for Fairfax County in Virginia. After a severe recession, the community's business leaders joined with the elected officials to "aid the County's economic recovery". Their challenges included:

* managing diverse inputs from elected and appointed officials, business leaders, university representatives and others.
* satisfying the needs of the strategic planning experts, the County Executive and the Commission Chair
* keeping people actively involved in a long meeting.

The resulting plan outlined goals and objectives as well as key strategies that both the governing body and the County staff need to follow in order to sustain a healthy economy.

Among the activities of the two day Electronic Meeting the nineteen commissioners in attendance generated 98 strategic internal strengths, which they discussed and placed into ten categories: location, quality of life, government, financial environment, economic climate, business community environment, education, infrastructure, human resources and public image. Working in small groups based on their areas of expertise they developed this list of strengths so that it could be used for developing a marketing plan to look for new business and community opportunities. In a similar way they analyzed weaknesses and developed actions to deal with them.

Feedback was very positive. Participants concluded that compared with a more traditional approach they were able to "produce more high-quality ideas, remain focused and progress further in their strategic planning process."

Strategic planning at national level

One of the more dramatic uses of Electronic Meetings has been in Sarajevo. The first facility, based on GroupSystems software, was opened in Sarajevo on April 3rd 1993, two days before the war started and the facility was destroyed. The replacement facility, funded by the Soros Foundation, opened in 1995, immediately after the Dayton Peace Accord was reached. Zlatko Lagumdzija has described how the plan for the new Management and Information Technologies (MIT) Center was developed under candlelight when there was no electrical power in Sarajevo.

As well as providing an educational tool for Government and business executives, the MIT Center has been used for strategic planning sessions at the city government and at national level. Visitors to the Electronic Meeting facilities have included both the President and Prime Minister of Bosnia-Herzegovina.

Also at country level, Noel Jones and Elizabeth Miller have run Electronic Meetings in two African countries on behalf of the World Bank. The objective was to gather input on World Bank strategies from a wide community, including Government officials, people from the public and private sector and tribal chiefs. In one of the countries over 120 stakeholders were in invited to Electronic Meetings, nine sessions being held in one week. The World Bank "ended up with a wealth of information" to develop a Country Assistance Strategy. Although many of the participants were new to this use of computers, 97% of the participants in one country and 100% of the participants in the second country "would recommend this technology to other groups".

Military strategic planning

The U.S. Air Force Information Resources Management used a multi-day Electronic Meeting to develop a strategic plan. Denise Shortt, the Re-engineering Team Leader in the Air Force Management Engineering Agency, facilitated the meeting, at the end of which 100% of the participants felt that the workshop had met its objective (in an anonymous vote). Most of the participants felt that the Electronic Meeting technology helped the group work more efficiently (81%) and effectively (89%).

The strategic plan required the consensus of three different functional communities, represented by 30 participants working on 20 PC's. Activities included performing a SWOT analysis (defining Strengths, Weaknesses, Opportunities and Threats), for which the participants were divided into four groups, using the Electronic Meeting facilities to quickly share and integrate the work of the groups.

The US Marine Corps has also been a wide user of Electronic Meetings under the leadership of General Don Lynch (now retired). For example, during a major re-organization the Facilities Department at Camp Pendleton felt that its role was exposed and that it needed to develop its mission by identifying opportunities for organizational and process improvement.

Using Electronic Meetings the Facilities Department developed a classical mission statement:

"to continually improve support for our customers by analyzing and recommending improvements to Facilities services and processes, and/or proposing organizational modifications to effectively/efficiently plan for, acquire, maintain, manage, operate and dispose of base infrastructure and facilities."

From this mission statement they developed a road map for redesigning the organization. Three teams used Electronic Meetings to finalize a new and successful organization.

The U.S. Air Force has developed strategic plans using Electronic Meetings. Mark Adkins and colleagues facilitated a structured planning process for the 366th Wing that "allowed a Wing of several thousand people to meet and develop a holistic strategic plan in less than three months". The 366th Wing is a 'composite' wing with both fighter and bomber planes. The Wing is composed of Groups, each Group is in turn composed of Squadrons, this hierarchy therefore requiring a well-integrated planning process in which hundreds of people were directly involved. The goals of the project included:

- improve the quality of the strategic plan
- reduce time to completion
- increase satisfaction with the strategic planning process
- increase commitment to implementation of the strategic plan.

The end results were action plans for each squadron. To monitor the effectiveness of the planning process, external Quality Improvement Officers evaluated these plans. This external evaluation "provides a strong indication that strategic plans created with computer support are higher in quality than those strategic plans produced without the use of GSS" (i.e. Electronic Meetings).

"In addition to the high quality, the computer-supported strategic plans addressed the Group's targets well and provided action plans that had a specific measurable. Squadrons that used the computer-supported strategic planning methodology saw an increase in satisfaction with the overall strategic planning process. Also there was a significant increase in the number of ideas generated and incorporated into the process, compared to traditional face-to-face strategic planning."

Scenario development

Michael Gardner of EDS has described the use of Electronic Meetings in scenario development sessions for General Motors. Gardner describes scenarios in this context as "a set of plausible and challenging stories about what might happen in the next 30 years". Scenarios are not forecasts – they do not predict by extrapolation, rather they are "mirrors of the unpredictable". A basic tenet of scenario planning is that "the future is shaped not only by the past, but by what we think is possible and what choices we make".

After preparation that included presentations by futurists and discussion of themes from relevant books, participants defined and prioritized probable drivers, trends and issues that could form the basis of likely scenarios. Up to 30 participants were involved, not all working on the same site. The network was extended into breakout rooms for group work. Lessons learned included:

• Electronic Meetings can speed up processes without losing content and participation
• Electronic Meetings can provide richer output
• there is a need to think beyond the traditional same time/same place environment.

On the specific issue of speeding up processes, Gardner reported that a full three-day agenda could be packed into two days – a very significant saving with this number of senior participants.

A rather different type of scenario development occurs in warfare analysis. Louis Gieszl and Richard Speigel of John Hopkins University used Electronic Meeting techniques for scenario development with experts from the US Navy. They found that Electronic Meetings added:

- natural, accurate collection of disparate views
- dynamic determination of consensus
- multiple levels of parallel conversations
- immediate feedback of results to participants.

Electronic Voting gave a poll of the participants' judgments on specific events. These votes were also used to highlight the issues that needed more discussion and resolution.

Involving everyone in the organization

The Danish company Oticon is a world leader in the manufacture of hearing aids and uses Electronic Meetings frequently. In one particular strategic planning exercise all employees were invited to contribute. The Managing Director, Lars Kolind, had initiated a re-organization that removed the traditional departments and job titles in order to create a 'network' organization.

In this new organization, described by Tom Peters in his book *Liberation Management*, Kolind created an environment where people were able to move into jobs or projects on a basis of what they would like to do and what they felt they could contribute. This is rather different from a conventional organization!

However, there were a number of potential paradoxes of this new organization and an Electronic Meeting was set up to ask the employees to address these paradoxes. The meeting was distributed across three locations within Denmark and 150 people participated. Examples of the paradoxes were:

• how to balance the wish for an open organization with the need for confidentiality towards the outside world
• how to provide career paths in a flat organization
• how to balance corporate economic results with the well-being of the employees.

Kolind's objectives from this type of open discussion were "to tap all the combined knowledge and creativity of our staff". By ensuring that "each and everyone contributed to the process of its birth" the new organization would be easier to implement.

Summary:

The examples in this chapter have shown that Electronic Meetings are an excellent solution for the challenges of strategic planning. Tangible results can be achieved more quickly than in conventional meetings. More people can be involved and their commitment to the strategy secured.

A strategic plan having been agreed, we now want to develop the appropriate business processes. The next chapter describes techniques for doing this using Electronic Meetings.

Chapter 5

BUSINESS PROCESS RE-ENGINEERING AND BENCHMARKING

Business process re-engineering (BPR) is the radical redesign of the activities of an organization in order to better achieve its goals. This includes a number of stages, each involving many people in the organization:

- gathering input on how processes work at present
- developing ideas for change and for new processes
- designing new processes and solutions
- gaining consensus and implementing the new processes.

Many organizations around the world are now using Electronic Meetings to develop solutions based on business process analysis and re-engineering.

Analyzing business processes

One successful approach, developed by consultant J. R. Holt, has been used many times, often with participants new to Electronic Meetings. The first stage is for the participants to input their view of:

- what is the organization doing right/what is working well?
- what is the organization doing wrong/what is not working?

This session may include input such as time study and other data that demonstrates either problems or successes. In order to help analyze the causes and possible solutions, the participants then divide their input into categories. Holt has used categories such as:

• business processes
• organizational culture
• computing technology.

In the next stage participants identify by Electronic Voting the most important items within each category. This prioritized list of items is then sorted into 'quick fix' or 'long term', where quick fix items are those requiring less than six months for resolution. Action plans are then defined for all items.

Figure 5.1 - Organizational culture issues from a business process re-engineering project (Holt)

Change the role of the lender:
- become a relationship manager
- spend more time outside the building
- focus on customer and customer service
- cross-selling
- have less administrative support

Change relationships of the departments
- break down boundaries and turfs
- change the definitions and scopes of jobs
- build team concepts
- look at structures and joint processes

Change the culture
- recognize the structure of the work
- be obsessed with Quality and efficiency
- invest in education and training
- empower employees to make decisions
- create a unity of purpose
- encourage finding faults with the system

Figure 5.1 above shows sample output in the category of 'organizational culture'. This project concerned the activities of the commercial representatives of a bank, where the Bank Productivity Department had identified that up to 75% of the representatives time was spent on non-revenue related activities.

Another example of the use of Electronic Meetings to analyze business processes is a project by Chevron Information Technology Company to standardize procurement processes throughout the company. Before being introduced to Electronic Meetings the Chevron project team had worked for a week analyzing and recording existing processes. Eight flip charts were covered with small sticky pieces of paper before the team came to the conclusion that the task was "unachievable" by

Figure 5.2 - Sample output of business process analysis for a procurement system (Wilkerson)

Procurement services
- Plan Procurement
  - Develop annual plan
    - determine materials and services needed for year
    - compile procurement req'ts for BU/HO teams
      - co-ordinate plan data from business units
      - develop individual customer purchase plans
      - summarize individual BU plans
    - list of commonly contracted materials/services
      - review project/maintenance plans
      - identify volume of work/materials
      - quantify $ for services for contract selection
    - get consensus on a list of contracts to develop
      - develop customer purchase plan req'ts
    - develop procurement strategies
      - define strategies available

manual means. Electronic Meetings came to the rescue, led by Chevron facilitator Ginny Wilkerson.

All the items on the flip charts, plus many additional items, were entered in the Electronic Meeting system and categorized. The resultant output was eight pages of single line items, arranged in a seven level hierarchy, containing 384 items in total. A sample of this output is shown in Figure 5.2. This list of items took 50 hours to complete, even using Electronic Meetings. The net result of the team's study was a saving of over $5 million per year to the company.

Electronic Meetings have been used to analyze business processes in a publishing company. Erik Lockhart of the Queen's Executive Decision Centre in Toronto helped his customer identify problem processes and improve them by:

• developing flow charts of existing processes
• evaluating current performance and assign appropriate color codes (red, yellow, green) according to status
• developing action plans for improvements
• revising the flow charts where necessary.

The team developed action plans to improve each of the processes that were classified as red, that is considered to be a poor performer. The team then documented the resources required for these actions, including their cost.

The US Army Construction Engineering Research Laboratories (USACERL) used Electronic Meetings in an intensive ten-week re-organization exercise. A committee of nine senior managers from the 1,000 strong organization met for four hours every day to accomplish this task. They started with the basic questions "what do we do?" and "who are our customers?". Input to these sessions came from e-mail as well as from the meeting participants.

Ginna Moore, an Electronic Meetings facilitator within USACERL, helped the committee analyze new organizational options by identifying criteria and constraints, including:

- responsiveness to customers
- flexibility
- effect on employee morale
- ability to attract funding
- no reduction in headcount.

The committee analyzed nine different organizational options and rated each option against the identified criteria. In this way they reduced the nine options to the three best options.

Since the records of Electronic Meetings were immediately available, the committee was able to maintain good communication with the 1,000 people in the organization by posting the minutes of each day's meeting onto the internal electronic Bulletin Board.

A new organization was agreed in ten weeks, an impressive time to do this while keeping one thousand people involved in the discussions. Electronic Meeting tools then helped assign teams to additional projects in identified areas.

Gail Corbitt and Lauren Wright of California State University used Electronic Meetings to analyze the order completion process of a large state agency. The process included order taking, order entry into the computer system, projection of delivery dates, order cancellation, customer inquiries and problem resolution. An initial review of the order completion process revealed the following problems:

- high staff turnover
- minimal training and development time
- a cumbersome paper flow process

- numerous delays and bottlenecks in word processing
- highly specialized job functions.

The project was completed in five phases:

1. focus groups to assess customer view of service quality
2. documentation of the current work flow
3. analysis of the current work flow
4. redesign of the work flow process
5. recommendations to implement the redesigned process.

In the focus groups customers were asked to help identify the problems and "had no trouble generating hundreds of comments in a very short time". These comments were grouped into seven categories and the customers were then asked for their ideas as to how to improve quality, thus keeping them involved in the improvement process.

The unambiguous customer feedback had a further positive benefit in giving senior management convincing evidence that changes were necessary, and hence enabling them to commit to the BPR project.

As a result of the project, during which Electronic Meetings were extensively used, the agency "was able to reduce the average time for order completion from 21 days prior to the process redesign to three days after the changes were implemented." The use of Electronic Meetings shortened the project timescale. For example, in the first phase one participant said, "we have just accomplished in five hours what took a team of 70 at our place six months to do meeting a full day every week"

Change Management in Government

Craig Petrun has described how Coopers and Lybrand (now PricewaterhouseCoopers) applied Electronic Meetings to facilitate change management efforts by the US Government. Petrun describes change management in this context as "the process of aligning the organization's people and culture with the changes in business strategy, organizational structure and systems".

A set of team activities was developed, based extensively on the use of Electronic Meetings. The main tasks were:

- develop a list of current service areas and functions
- map strategy goals to current service areas
- construct list of key organizational change questions
- review best practices (input received from comparable organizations)
- review service areas and prioritize
- develop list of recommended changes to the reward systems
- develop detailed recommendations for each issue
- develop three alternative models for new organizational structure
- summarize lessons learned for future organizational team efforts.

Petrun used Electronic Voting to make sure that the team was in agreement. He gives the following useful definition of consensus:

"By *consensus* we do not mean unanimity of opinion. A consensus is where each group member has had adequate and fair input to influence the decision of the group. Individual members may not view the decision as their preferred decision, but they can live with it and have ownership of it, such that they can advocate and implement it."

The project reaching the following conclusions:

- GroupSystems and its anonymous input capabilities significantly enhance the change management process (GroupSystems is software for Electronic Meetings)
- GroupSystems significantly reduces required meeting time, but not decision making time
- the use of GroupSystems tools should not replace the use of verbal discussions during the attainment of consensus.

Benchmarking

In a benchmarking study, organizations compare their processes. Comparison with direct competitors can be difficult, but non-competitive organizations can usually be found with whom to compare selected processes. Supermarket chains for example have efficient stock control systems from which manufacturing companies might learn. These comparisons can give valuable pointers as to which processes have good potential for improvement.

A benchmarking study using Electronic Meeting techniques was carried out by 12 hospitals geographically dispersed across the United States. The purpose of this study, by the Chenault group, was to:

- discover what worked well
- discover what did not work well
- make adjustments to help hospitals move from what did not work well to what worked well.

The steps in this benchmarking study were:

- survey 18 critical functional areas
- make function by function comparisons
- arrange face to face exchanges
- capture the comments
- evaluate and define best practices.

For example when analyzing waiting time in emergency rooms, each hospital tracked waiting times, and graphed them for distribution to the other participants. One of the rules of benchmarking is that you have to expose your own performance, even if it is less than perfect!

All the participants in the study used Electronic Meetings to exchange comments on these results and to analyze the processes used. Electronic Voting helped select the best practices, evaluated for impact on cost, quality and speed.

Summary:

Electronic Meetings are being used extensively in business process re-engineering as well as in benchmarking. Electronic Meetings reduce project timescales and costs and in some cases make the difference between failure and success.

Another important aspect of running a successful organization is to manage relationships with suppliers. Electronic Meetings are of course being used in this area.

Chapter 6

SUPPLIER MANAGEMENT

Many organizations spend between 60% or more of gross income with suppliers (or vendors). Furthermore, in these days of what Business Week has described as 'virtual corporations', suppliers and business partners are increasingly involved in the core business of an organization. Many suppliers of large organizations provide goods and services directly to the organization's customers. Hence a good supplier management system is essential.

Yet managing suppliers effectively is becoming more difficult as more people in the organization have contact with them. Each person may have something useful to contribute in assessing and managing the supplier. Using Electronic Meetings, it is possible to collect all the relevant input and build a complete picture from which to manage suppliers to the optimum benefit of the organization.

Vendor selection

The Information Systems Department of the University of Texas M. D. Anderson Cancer Center used Electronic Meetings in the process of vendor selection. The Department needed to arrange contracts with a pool of vendors to provide high quality, low cost computing support.

The existing process for negotiating with suppliers took too long to complete, in part because the public nature of the institution required that certain formal procedures be followed. This time delay was such that some good suppliers would not work with the Department. Joy Rizzi helped the Center apply Electronic Meetings to solve the problem.

The first preparation stage was a face to face Electronic Meeting lasting about one hour to determine the following:

- which vendors were to be included in the process
- the evaluation criteria to be used in Electronic Voting
- weighted measures for these evaluation criteria.

The evaluation criteria used to assess the competing vendors included:

- costs, for which there were standard formulae
- vendor personnel, their initiative, degree of training, stability and quality
- vendor staffing, breadth and depth of personnel
- references, using a standard formula and personal experiences
- discretionary, i.e. the quality of the proposal, personal experiences and other information.

Some of this data, such as past performance and financial status, was on computer systems. For other data quite lengthy proposals had to be analyzed by different people at different times. Hence the optimum way to summarize the data was to run a *different time/different place* Electronic Meeting. In this way data could be input continuously and the participants in the exercise could always see the latest status.

When all this data had been entered, a face to face Electronic Meeting lasting about four hours was held to reach a consensus on the rating of the vendors. The vendors that came out the best at this stage were interviewed and some ratings were adjusted. At the end of this process there was a list of acceptable vendors.

The process was sufficiently clear and documented to be acceptable to the auditors.

This process of supplier assessment using Electronic Meetings can in principle be applied by any organization. Figure 6.1 gives the flow of the process showing the type of Electronic Meeting.

Figure 6.1 - Process for vendor evaluation (Rizzi)

Activity	Meeting type
Develop invitations to bid	
Check proposals as received	
Evaluate the proposals	*different time/different place*
Enter financial and other data	*different time/different place*
Achieve consensus	*face to face*
Interview leading vendors	
Final selection	*face to face*

Rizzi identified the following advantages from using Electronic Meetings to assess vendors:

- consistency was achieved by clearly defining the criteria
- the most appropriate people participated in the evaluation because the different time/different place Electronic Meetings allowed them flexibility in timing
- more people were able to participate in the evaluation
- Electronic Voting improved the quality of the ratings, since the evaluators were urged to discuss their ratings and adjust if necessary in order to reach consensus
- evaluators were consistently prepared and more productive in the face to face meetings, since these were not scheduled until all the preparation had been completed in the different time/different place meetings.

Another example of using Electronic Meetings to solve a vendor selection problem was in Fairfax County, Virginia, where two vendors were competing for a large contract for a new student information database. Carol Lindsay and Nikki Thomas-Campbell describe how each product offering was rated against 17 objectives, each objective having 8 – 25 sub-objectives. The Selection Advisory Committee needed to quickly assess the products, document their vote justifications and produce clear comparative results, Matrix Voting was the obvious tool to use, with the following voting choices:

M = Meets or exceeds requirements
F = Falls short of requirements
U = Unavailable or not demonstrated.

The results were accumulated in a spreadsheet and the total final results were available at the end of the meeting. Thus a far more comprehensive analysis was possible than could ever have been achieved by conventional assessment processes. Using Electronic Meetings was judged to be "very useful in helping the participants to organize their thoughts/ideas/questions etc." "The use of this facility enhanced the professional approach to this project."

Vendors collaborating

At first sight, an organization might feel concerned if its vendors are working closely together. However, there are times when this can stimulate effective competition and better solutions, one such occasion being when the Office of the Assistant Secretary of Defense for Health Affairs established a vendor consortium to develop a clinical lexicon. The lexicon is to allow Health Care Professionals to view information across multiple information systems in a consistent medical view as well as providing a common vocabulary between the DoD and external organizations. This is clearly an issue with considerable health and cost implications. A framework was needed where competing vendors could work together effectively under the following broad principles:

- open discussion with no secrets
- qualified, empowered team members
- consistent, success-oriented, proactive participation
- continuous 'up-the-line' communication
- reasoned disagreement
- issues raised and resolved early.

A series of Electronic Meetings provided this framework, as described by Carolyn Cukierman of Battelle. E-mail and the Web were used to distribute copies of meeting reports. The project concluded with a successful proof-of-concept demonstration to the Assistant Secretary of Defense for Health Affairs. All the team members "agreed that the use of EMS was a critical success factor in managing the work of the team".

Managing tenders

The Danish company National Procurement used Electronic Meetings to help streamline their process for managing tenders. National Procurement is jointly owned by the Danish government and the Danish National Association of Local Authorities, with a mission to supply efficient procurement for public authorities and organizations. A Web server makes information available across the Internet to would-be suppliers and also enables them to enter their tender information to the assessment process. Electronic Meetings play a key role, firstly in ensuring that important information about suppliers and products is appropriately shared and checked, and secondly in the evaluation process itself. In the evaluation process Matrix Voting is used to score suppliers and products, based on criteria that can be individually weighted by the assessment team.

This decision model can handle many different analyses, e.g. to develop a two-by-two matrix of product quality vs. supplier quality, enabling National Procurement to identify the high quality products that come from high quality suppliers. The model is also useful in a supply area where it is possible to purchase a product from different suppliers, where some of the would-be suppliers are also dealers and where there is also interdependence between some of the products.

Finally the use of Electronic Meetings ensures that the evaluation process is fully documented. The end result, as described by Erik Svaneborg and Vagn Andersen of National Procurement with Chris Mora-Jensen of [inno:vasion], is an efficient and standardized electronic tendering process.

Summary:

Summarizing the components of supplier/vendor performance, including numeric records and many individual opinions, can be done extremely effectively within Electronic Meetings. This can have benefits for most organizations.

The next chapter looks at the contribution that Electronic Meetings can make to managing risks and keeping the organization on track.

Chapter 7

QUALITY AND RISK MANAGEMENT

One might hope that having established customer requirements, developed a winning strategy, sorted out the business processes and chosen the best suppliers, as described in the four previous chapters, life would now be plain sailing. Not so, of course.

Firstly there are risks that must be managed if the organization is to keep to its plan. Risks are getting more complex and more expensive to deal with, as some recent spectacular business failures have shown. Secondly, once the business processes are set up, quality levels must be maintained and continually increased. This chapter will show how these two issues, risk management and quality, are being tackled using Electronic Meetings.

Managing Risk

PricewaterhouseCoopers in the UK have pioneered the use of Electronic Meetings to help organizations manage the business risks that they face. In PricewaterhouseCoopers' Control Risk Self Assessment workshops, participants identify business risks, assess their impact and develop action plans to deal with them.

Firstly, the participants review and agree on the business objectives of the department or organization. This sets the base line against which to consider risks. The participants then enter all the risks that they can identify within the business area being covered, the use of anonymity helping to ensure complete openness. The risks may be grouped into categories. The next stage is a vote on the risks under two criteria:

- the likelihood of the risk occurring
- the scale of impact of the risk.

There may be differences of opinion between the participants; these will be clearly highlighted by analyzing the spread of votes (see Chapter 14). Participants then record what controls are already in place for these risks, starting with the high likelihood, high impact risks.

PricewaterhouseCoopers have run many such workshops, usually lasting a half or full day. The full record of the meeting, with all the comments and risks that have been entered is a valuable audit document. Actions that have been agreed are clearly documented.

Frank Hailstones, a Senior Partner of PricewaterhouseCoopers Internal Audit Services Partner, says that use of Electronic Meetings "has significantly improved the productivity of workshops compared to conventional approaches".

National Grid, which owns and operates the electricity transmission system in England and Wales, also uses Electronic Meetings very effectively in risk management. Bob Dudley, Manager of Operational Risk, reports that his principle challenge is fulfilling user demand, a pleasant situation for an audit department!

Failure Mode Effect Analysis (FMEA)

Similar in some respects to risk analysis, Failure Mode Effect Analysis (FMEA) is a well established tool containing a number of systematic activities to determine potential sources of failure in a product or a process, to evaluate the possible effects of such failure and to develop an action plan for their elimination or reduction.

In other words, FMEA asks, 'what could go wrong?', a question that may have been overlooked as the product or process is designed, when there is generally a focus on what happens when everything goes well, and a rush to get into production as soon as the design is completed. Hence FMEA's have to be completed quickly. Participants in an FMEA must be encouraged to submit freely a wide range of possible ideas, so a lot of input is created that has to be managed and carefully documented. Obviously a case for Electronic Meetings!

Ellen Shafer and Mary Jo Csonka have applied Electronic Meeting technology to a standardized form of FMEA developed by Ford, General Motors and Chrysler. The use of Electronic Meeting technology was found to be "a swift, practical and effective approach" to completing the FMEA process. The client who had requested the service "reports that it was a much more effective way to complete the necessary FMEAs required of them".

Ideally people from different skills, backgrounds and departments should be involved in an FMEA in order to get maximum input of ideas. This suggests the use of distributed Electronic Meetings, where subject matter experts and other external participants can conveniently contribute to an FMEA without the time and cost of travel.

Quality self-assessment

It is said that the quest for Quality never ends because more improvement is always possible. If the search for Quality is unending, there are some widely acknowledged measures of progress, including:

- ISO 9000 certification
- the Malcolm Baldrige Award in the United States
- the European Foundation for Quality Management Award (EFQM).

Apart from battling for external recognition, many organizations are adapting these different measures of Quality as internal self-assessment tools. Thus they can measure and accelerate Quality programs at project and department level, as well as at company level.

For internal self-assessment the people in the department concerned carry out the measuring process themselves, not external assessors. The self-assessment then naturally leads to a committed action plan for improvements.

Bernard Martin at the IBM International Education Center in Belgium applied techniques of Electronic Meetings to the Quality self-assessment process. The first stage in the process is to list and agree existing strengths and weaknesses. All the members of the department give their input flagging it with a (-) or a (+) to show whether the point is a strength or a weakness (a weakness is more positively called an 'area for improvement'). When the participants are agreed on the positive and negative points, they vote on what they think should be the score of the department under each heading. Since all the individuals record their opinions anonymously, the group can do a thorough and honest analysis of its performance.

For example, one section of the Baldrige Award deals with 'Knowledge of Customer Requirements and Expectations'. Under this heading should be described 'how the company determines current and future customer requirements and expectations'. Figure 7.1 illustrates possible input for training organization.

Figure 7.1 - Input of customer requirements and expectations

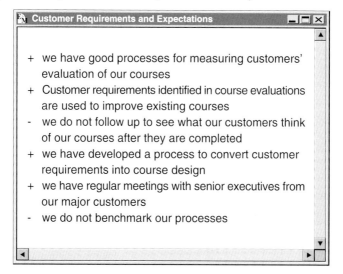

Hence the group can come to agreement about its rating. This rating can then be used to measure future improvements and also for comparison with other departments.

Professor Milton Chen at San Diego State University has also used Electronic Meetings for Baldrige Quality self-assessment. He has conducted a number of sessions for commercial and military organizations with significant business results. His focus is to obtain consensus from the evaluation team on:

• description of total quality implementation
• strengths and areas for improvement
• what score is appropriate for each criteria item
• priority actions for next period with ratings.

Teams usually consist of about a dozen members of upper and middle management. Chen finds that one of the benefits is to make all team members aware of what other parts of the organization are doing, since some participants seem to feel that the organization as a whole should have a rating based solely on the performance of their department! The self-assessment sessions allow an organization to examine all departments and make an overall rating of their quality system management. They also allow organizations to spread the most efficient and successful practices within the entire corporation. For a company that is interested in applying for a Quality Award, the self-assessment assists in the application planning.

Chen sees further application of this technique to various performance evaluations required by U.S. Governmental Departments for their self-assessment.

Summary:

Risk Management and Quality are essential management tools identifying what might go wrong or what might inhibit us from achieving outstanding results. Electronic Meetings are ideal for both approaches. Anonymity encourages the creative idea generation that is required, while the Electronic Voting tools ensure the consensus and support of people involved to make sure the issues are tackled.

The next chapter looks at how the field of Human Resource Management is benefiting from Electronic Meetings.

Chapter 8

HUMAN RESOURCE MANAGEMENT

Electronic Meetings have a particular significance for those activities that are conventionally encompassed within the phrase Human Resources. In the previous five chapters Electronic Meetings have been seen as a tool that makes it easier, quicker and cheaper to define and implement organizational solutions. For Human Resource Management by contrast, Electronic Meetings are more than just a cost-effective tool.

Electronic Meetings can actually impact the culture of an organization by putting into action the so frequently used words 'we want to involve our people', 'people are our most important asset', 'we need everybody's contribution', and perhaps most importantly 'our managers are leaders, not administrators'.

Apart from their potential impact on the organization's culture Electronic Meetings are making a specific contribution in many areas of Human Resource Management, including:

- people assessment
- group counseling
- opinion surveys
- health and safety
- skills management
- negotiating
- teamwork and trust building
- multi-cultural issues.

People assessment

In the painful situation that a small company needed to cut its staff by about 30%, it was particularly important to have a fair process for assessing people. Carol Flament and Norman Rose set up an Electronic Meeting for the supervisors.

Supervisors had prepared evaluations of their own people on a five-point scale. However, since most of the supervisors knew most of the people concerned, they decided to develop a collective opinion using an Electronic Meeting. In this meeting, they shared their knowledge about the people and came to a consensus on their assessments.

Comments about people had to be fact-based, using first hand experience and specific examples (no anonymity at this stage). Senior Managers had the right to overrule the ratings, as the supervisors had clearly understood from the beginning of the exercise. Figure 8.1 shows the factors used in the evaluation.

Figure 8.1 - Factors used in personnel evaluation

Behavioral skills
- puts the customer first
- makes informed decisions
- achieves results

Team working
- leads with vision and purpose
- fosters teamwork
- communicates openly and effectively

Personal
- promotes diversity
- develops self and others
- improves continuously

Technical knowledge and skills

But how to evaluate the supervisors? At the M. D. Anderson Cancer Center, Houston, the Director of Patient Care asked just that question and in this case, the employees evaluated the supervisors. The first stage was for the Director and the supervisors to develop 20 evaluation statements in an Electronic Meeting. The employees then voted on an agree/disagree basis on each evaluation statement for each supervisor. After the vote session, the employees were able to enter comments about the supervisors, but were not able to see the comments made by other employees.

The Director of Patient Care received a full package of all results for each supervisor, and each supervisor received their combined vote results and the comments made about them. The Director said that the Electronic Meetings were invaluable in illuminating previously vague employee-supervisor problems, employees having been reluctant to come forward with problems because they did not want to be identified as non-team players. The anonymity of the Electronic Meetings made the quality and objectivity of the evaluations possible

Group counseling

To allow people to make anonymous comments on others and then to use these comments for employment and career decisions may cause concern to some people, and clearly such Electronic Meetings must be carefully managed. However, Electronic Meetings have been used in an environment of significantly greater personal sensitivity than a commercial organization. Mark Huber of Wake Forest University and Alan Dennis of the University of Georgia have used Electronic Meetings in a men's counseling group. Counseling groups "strive to create a safe place which supports the communication and resolution of deeply personal issues, e.g. frustration with societal status quo, sexuality, etc". The formation of the group was advertised on campus and in the local community. Participants were screened prior to the first meeting and individuals whose problems were inappropriate for this group were referred elsewhere. There were seven members in the group, including two experienced counselors. An additional person operated the Electronic Meeting technology. Ages ranged from 25 to 52 years. The group met weekly, ten times for two hours.

Huber and Dennis concluded, "the counselors and the participants felt that the use of GSS enhanced the overall counseling process" (GSS, Group Support System, in this context is equivalent to an Electronic Meeting). They would "recommend that counselors and others who attempt to facilitate the discussion of sensitive and emotional issues consider using a GSS".

Health and Safety

Health and Safety is clearly an area that requires open discussion of ideas and the development of active consensus, as can be provided by Electronic Meetings. This was illustrated in an Electronic Meeting run by Tony Mason of Halliburton, Brown and Root on behalf of the offshore oil industry in the North Sea. The offshore safety sector had a pan-industry board to advise the UK Health and Safety Executive on the most appropriate areas for offshore safety research and to monitor progress of research projects. The sector having undergone changes in both funding and organization, it was felt to be appropriate to review the advisory board's remit and constitution. The board represented all parties in the offshore industry, thus it was paramount that there be a genuinely consultative process in gathering views on current status and future directions. The industry partners used an Electronic Meeting to establish a consensus view. This enabled the gathering of views under different topics and the prioritizing of effort, e.g. which research areas demanded the most immediate attention and appropriate share of the budget.

The report of the meeting summarized the views for presentation to the rest of the research strategy board. The next step was to widen the debate further and use Electronic Meetings to garner views from the other industry members, so that further restructuring was truly representative.

Skills Management

An Electronic Meeting was used by some members of the European Foundation for Management Development who wanted to improve their skills management systems by exchanging information with each other. The participants at the meeting each wanted to know how the other organizations were progressing, but in public no-one was going to make any less than positive remarks about their own performance and their own organization. However if everyone gave the smooth presentation of a public relations officer there would be little useful dialogue.

An Electronic Meeting enabled an open and structured exchange of information without anyone having to give away family secrets. The sequence of the meeting was simple. After an introduction to Electronic Meetings, the participants discussed and responded to a set of pre-prepared open-ended questions.

The first question put to the group was:

Have senior executives demonstrated a real commitment to employees' skill development?

In public the answer is of course 'yes'. But what was the answer under the cover of anonymity? The answers included:

- 'yes' 9 times, complete with supporting information
- 'no' twice
- 'unanswerable' once.

So here in an elapsed time of about five minutes was valuable feedback that a significant majority of companies really have committed to manage their skill development. The supporting information gave new ideas for the participants to share, and there was ammunition to take home for those who had felt obliged to answer 'no'.

There are differences between words and action. So the next question was:

Is there a senior executive in charge of skill strategy?

Instantly there was a drop in the number of 'yes' replies. But wait a minute, even if an executive is appointed:

Is this executive measured on the results of the skill strategy?

and another good question to test the water...

How often has this responsibility changed in the last year?

and even:

Is there a separate budget for skills development?

Hence the meeting was now able to explore in depth the extent of any real commitment to skills development - and the majority of companies were still giving essentially positive answers.

Moving on from what senior executives should be doing to what the participants of the meeting should be doing:

Have you defined the core skills necessary to meet the business objectives of your organization, i.e. those skills that must remain internal to the company?

There were almost unanimously positive answers to this question. So let us probe a little:

Do you have a documented skills development process?

And:

Is your skills development process linked to market segments?

And:

How do you measure increase in skill levels and relate this to the skills gap?

It appeared that most companies, in spite of having defined their core skills, did not have a process to link core skills to the market place, that is to make sure that the list of core skills was kept up-to-date with changing market requirements. No company thought it had a really effective means of relating the company skill requirement to individuals' skills, as measured for example at performance appraisals.

Another interesting question in these days of virtual corporations and supplier partnerships...

Do you have a skills inventory for business partners and external workforce partners?

Almost unanimously, no. Finally:

Do you have an executive communication plan to make sure that employees and customers realize the value you place on skill development?

And:

How do you reward people in your organization for acquiring skills?

Not a lot of positive replies to these two questions, but again some useful ideas. All answers were immediately seen by the participants, who were then able to make additional comments. All questions and answers were printed and distributed at the end of the meeting. In an elapsed time of about 90 minutes, a useful and confidential exchange of ideas and activities was possible - within an Electronic Meeting. The value of the discussion to the participants was confirmed by an anonymous survey at the end of the meeting.

Negotiating using Electronic Meetings

Bruce Herniter and others have described the use of Electronic Meetings to improve the efficiency of negotiations between employers and unions. During the main negotiation sessions, a facilitator typed much of the record of the discussion into the system. This saved the participants some effort and allowed them to concentrate on the negotiation proposals. The accuracy of what the facilitator typed was guaranteed by its instant public display.

Each party in the negotiations had a private room with a PC linked to the network. Thus during its private discussions each party could review the total and accurate record of what had been said in the meeting so far. Each party could also prepare further material in its private room for submission when the Electronic Meeting reconvened, thus saving time and increasing the clarity of communication.

Erran Carmel, Bruce Herniter and Jay Nunamaker have described using Electronic Meetings in actual negotiation between:

- a bus company and the Union
- between a non-profit health facility and the American Federation of State County Municipal Employees.

Roger Fisher and William Ury describe four key points of negotiation in their bestseller book *Getting to Yes*:

1. separate the people from the problem
2. focus on interest, not positions
3. invent options for mutual gain
4. insist on using objective criteria.

It is evident that this method can adapt well to Electronic Meetings. Anonymity will separate the people from the problem (Point 1), and will also allow participants to focus on interests, not positions (Point 2). An *interest* in this context is specific, while a *position* is more general. For example an organization might demand a price reduction of a specified percentage from a supplier, which would represent a *position*. However the *interest* of the organization might be expressed as 'more efficient operation', and this could perhaps be achieved by different packaging, more frequent deliveries or a number of creative ideas that could benefit the customer to the same extent as a price cut. For Point 3, Electronic Meetings provide an excellent environment for inventing and assessing new options. Point 4, use of objective criteria, can be achieved with the voting techniques available in Electronic Meetings.

Teamwork and trust building

The introduction of teamwork is usually seen as a means of improving productivity on the basis that a successful team can achieve more than the sum of individual efforts. Yet many managers may feel that, apart from exhortation, they can make relatively little contribution to helping people work successfully in teams. Electronic Meetings allow the free exchanges of ideas and opinions that help change a group into a team.

For example, Erik Lockhart of Queen's Executive Decision Centre, Toronto, has used Electronic Meetings for team building. In one case the objective of the Electronic Meeting was to assign individual responsibilities and tasks to the Management team of a paperwork plant. The team had become conscious that some management jobs not being done while other jobs had too many people working on them. The steps in the meeting were:

- identify tasks
- define who is doing the tasks now
- agree who should do the tasks
- compare these two models
- assign tasks accordingly

Figure 8.2 - Sample management task assignments

Production Supervisor
- coach supervisors on 5 minute safety rules
- maintain control charts for compilation
- investigate Customer Service Rep complaints
Process Services Supervisor
- calculate monthly Quality statistics
- update Quality Control testing accuracy
- perform monthly TQM coaching sessions
Mill Superintendent
- complete weekly operator scheduling
- meet with Union reps daily
- evaluate supervisors and crew

Figure 8.2 illustrates some of the new task assignments. The members of the management team assigned the tasks among themselves using Matrix Voting.

Lockhart also worked with a Crisis Centre Emergency Response Team, ten social workers who wanted to improve their teamwork. The task of the Electronic Meetings was to review team functioning and to create an ideal team model. The team listed adjectives that described their ideal team and then defined an opposite to each adjective. This gave them five 'dimensions' on which to assess themselves on a scale of 1 to 10.

Figure 8.3 shows the five 'dimensions' of teamwork. Having agreed the team's position on these dimensions, they worked individually to propose one action for each dimension that would move the team toward the ideal image. The final stage was to discuss and commit to these proposals.

In another exercise, Lockhart found that mixing adventure-based activities such as high rope events with Electronic Meetings was a powerful stimulus to team building.

Figure 8.3 - Five dimensions of a team (Lockhart)

Fragmented	Cohesive
Autocratic	Participative
Ignorant	Knowledgeable
Unproductive	Effective
Untrustworthy	Trustworthy

Teamwork is not only an internal exercise within a small group. Perhaps as important is the teamwork between different groups of people, and few issues can be more important than looking after children in the care of the community. Carol Lindsay has described how Electronic Meetings were used in Fairfax County, Virginia to improve working relationships between two agencies providing services to children placed in court care.

The two agencies were the Department of Social Services' Court Supervised Care unit and the Mental Health Services unit. The formation of new interagency/citizen teams had changed the child placement process and each agency needed to rethink how it worked.

Representatives of the two agencies participated in a series of Electronic Meetings. In one meeting, one of the agencies described the services needed for the children it was responsible for, and the other unit identified the services it could provide. Another joint activity in an Electronic Meeting was to list the activities in the typical day of workers in the two units. "For the first time, both groups realized they shared common experiences, felt similar doubts and concerns; both desired to protect and care for the same children".

"The use of (Electronic Meetings) between the two agencies resulted in an increased understanding of each others' working environment, improved relationship among staff, improved staff morale, all of which had a direct positive effect on improving services to the children placed in court care."

And that's teamwork!

However, teamwork can be more difficult to maintain when Electronic Meetings are run between multiple different sites. Daniel Mittleman, Robert Briggs and Nicholas Romano of the University of Arizona have run many distributed Electronic Meetings, both 'same time' and 'different time'. They have observed that distributed team members have less opportunity for team building and find it more difficult to converge to decisions than if all the meeting participants are on the same site. Remote team members may even perceive that the facilitator or meeting owner is biased towards any participants who may be co-located with them. Actions to be taken to counteract such feelings include being very explicit about the objectives of the meeting and how the agenda is constructed to achieve these objectives. Distributed participants should have a real vested interest in the outcome of the meeting and the business reasons for holding a distributed meeting should be clear to all concerned.

Multi-cultural Electronic Meetings

Frances Teti of Team Dynamics Associates facilitated an Electronic Meeting for a Property and Casualty Insurance Company on the subject of Workforce Diversity. Although the company's profile of statistics showed tremendous management support for a diverse workforce, many situations were coming to the surface indicating that minorities of all types were not full participants in the corporate culture. As Teti describes:

"The issue they faced was not knowing for sure what level of sensitivity existed and how willing the participants would be to having an open and candid conversation on their concerns and needs. How could they open up the dialogue among employees and between employees and management?"

The HR team wanted to uncover the major inhibitors to all employees and managers being comfortable together. From an Electronic Meeting they received:

• a narrative document containing (anonymous) dialogue on the current status of diversity
• responses to a survey on how managers felt about their working environment
• a dialogue on what further staff development was required
• a list of diversity issues affecting the environment
• a discussion on the diversity mentoring program
• a prioritized list of issues for the corporation to address.

The session was therefore an "open and powerful forum for idea exchange and the confronting of real issues".

Dave Philips and Debbie Basha of Soza & Company have experience of hundreds of Electronic Meetings and point out that as well as the more apparent national and language cultures, differences in business culture must also be considered. Their experience includes for example a strategic planning session for 230 participants in a newly formed organization, the Pennsylvania Mapping and Geological Information Consortium, with 25 working groups in single room. Other Electronic Meeting based assignments included a job training assessment for the United States Coast Guard, working for the Puerto Rico Public Housing Administration and a one day workshop of 200 people for the Council of Governments in Central Pennsylvania. People running Electronic Meetings need to be able to relate to different cultures, particularly when there are multiple languages to take account of. It is important to stay flexible and to be able to adapt the flow of the Electronic Meeting as required.

Kathleen Kelly of GlobalTech Alliances has used Electronic Meetings to run training exercises in intercultural awareness. Kelly presents scenarios to participants and asks for their anonymous comments under open ended headings such as:

• What meaning did you attribute to these behaviors?
• What values are at work here?
• How can this situation be resolved?

This has proved an effective way of bringing culture and diversity issues into the open, without putting pressure in the individuals involved.

Summary:

Electronic Meetings are being successfully applied in a wide variety of HR functions, including performance assessment, opinion surveys, Health and Safety, skills management, team development and diversity training. There are enormous immediate benefits to be gained.

On a wider HR front Electronic Meetings have the potential to give organizations a more open and creative culture. HR managers who are looking for such a culture change could benefit by promoting the introduction of Electronic Meetings.

Closely related to the HR Department is Education and Training. Let us look in the next chapter at how Electronic Meetings can improve this function.

Chapter 9

EDUCATION AND TRAINING

Some aspects of adult education and training are similar to a conventional meeting:

- a group of people are exchanging knowledge and opinions
- many participants do not have the opportunity to make a significant contribution
- the effective result of the session is often not clear.

Given such similarities, it is not surprising that Electronic Meetings are making a significant contribution in Education and Training.

Adult training in industry and commerce

Increasingly individuals are personally responsible for keeping their skills relevant and up to date. It is therefore natural that people attending training courses will expect to give frequent feedback and have a degree of control over the course content.

Electronic Meeting technology is of course ideal to achieve this level of feedback, quickly and easily. Participants can be asked at the beginning of the course if the objectives are clear and appropriate. Feedback during the course can be maintained with a simple set of questions such as:

- Any comments on the last session?
- What did you learn in the last session?
- Any particular requirements for the next session?
- Do you feel you are making good progress toward achieving the objectives of the course?

The answers to such questions will ensure that the course keeps in line with the requirements of the participants. This is a situation where it can be useful not to let participants see each others comments initially, so that everyone gives their views independently (this technique is described in Chapter 12).

The responses to the question "What did you learn?" are useful both for teacher and student. The teacher can see how the whole class is progressing and each student can see how they compare with the rest of the class without risk of personal exposure.

Feedback to speakers

Electronic Meeting technology is also used to prioritize questions and comments to speakers during presentations and conferences. The audience enters questions and comments onto their PC's during the presentation, which the speaker can then address at the end of the presentation. At a later stage, the speaker can type in responses to all the questions and comments. These responses can then be printed out and distributed to the audience.

Hence the speaker gets the opportunity to address the important questions and comments from the audience as a whole, not just those from the first couple of people to jump to their feet. The immediacy of the feedback also encourages the speaker to keep the presentation interesting and to the point!

Robert Davison of City University, Hong Kong and Robert Briggs of the University of Arizona, have reported on a number of uses of Electronic Meeting technology in this way, including at a British Commonwealth conference of 50 officials from 24 countries. Participants needed to be reassured that typing during a presentation was not disruptive. Participant comments included:

"I like the ease with which the system allows people to voice comments that they wouldn't otherwise voice."

"I would have left after the morning sessions if it were not for the opportunity to input ideas with the others."

Electronic Meetings in Business Schools

Professor Doug Vogel at the University of Arizona has run more than a thousand Electronic Meetings and regularly uses the technology with students around the world. In one instance, Vogel and Professor Maryan Alavi of the University of Maryland ran joint classes for business students. The classes at opposite ends of the country met as one, with students asking questions of both professors and sharing the responses. This long-distance class was a valuable learning experience that included an effective and memorable introduction to today's business world.

Professor Albert Angehrn of INSEAD, the European Institute of Business Administration in Fontainebleu, France, has used different time/different place Electronic Meetings with post-graduate and industrial students for business games. He concludes that while face-to-face mode is still perceived as key in top management meetings and highly political environments, "meeting efficiency can be effectively achieved through Electronic Meetings".

Professor Graham Pervan and colleagues at the University of Curtin in Western Australia have used Electronic Meetings to help address issues of low morale where there is a poor match between the values of the organization and those of the individuals within it. Organizational members are asked to generate:

(a) their own values
(b) their perceptions of the organization's values.

Electronic Meetings help to do this with parallel input and by providing the anonymity which individuals find helpful in expressing their true feelings. The lists from (a) and (b) can then be compared to identify how well matched they are and to help the organization find ways of improving the match where necessary.

At Henley Management College in the UK Elspeth McFadzean and Jane McKenzie have been using Electronic Meetings in the Decision Support Centre for several years, particularly in combination with creativity techniques. One technique used in a strategic planning session was 'object stimulation', where the participants were asked to think of a company that in their view produced a high quality service. They were then asked to enter what they thought were the reasons for this high quality. Because each participant thought of different companies, ranging from the local pub to multinational companies, the ideas they produced were varied and novel. The facilitator then asked the group to relate these ideas back to their own organization. Hence a number of very innovative ideas were developed and expanded upon. One manager commented "We would never have thought of so many ideas if we had undertaken this manually. Moreover, we had the freedom to think creatively and outrageously because the system was anonymous. I am very pleased with what we have produced".

Supporting the University Faculty

Barbara O'Brian and Alice Renner of Wright State University, College of Nursing have used Electronic Meetings on a regular basis. Among the issues that have been addressed are:

- Obtaining college faculty input for university strategic planning within a one-week deadline. A report with input from all faculty members was prepared within this tight timescale.
- Identifying questions to be asked in a research study on congestive heart failure. In one hour 171 questions were listed and sorted into 11 categories. A printed report was available at the close of the meeting.
- Obtaining consultation from 14 national experts on the data elements to be included in the patient core data set. A critique of 65 data elements was produced in a 78-page report. "The experts loved the method".
- A simulation in a health policy class for graduate nursing students on ethical issues involving euthanasia. This stimulated a rich discussion; the evaluation indicated that the students felt this was a valuable exercise.

Conrad Røyksund, Mari Montri Heltne and Liang Chee Wee at Luther College, Iowa, have used their Electronic Meeting room to gather input from faculty, staff and students in exploring academic issues for the college in the 21st Century. This included meetings of the Board of Regents Technology Task Force, planning an organizational merger and a series of meetings on the issues of faculty governance. Weekly meetings addressed such issues as:

- What are the major responsibilities of faculty in the governance structure?
- What is working well in the current structure?

- What is least effective in the current structure?

The resulting proposal for a new governance structure including reducing the number of committees from 17 to seven with drastically reduced size of committees. This proposal had considerable buy-in because faculty felt that they had been part of the process.

Maureen Lynch and Bill Wood of the University of South Australia have used Electronic Meetings so that students could give feedback and evaluation of courses. There were specific problems with the traditional evaluation using questionnaires:

- a rating does not indicate what the problems are
- many students ignore the section in the questionnaire asking for free format comments
- below average feedback to a lecturer is simply depressing if it is not accompanied with constructive criticism
- questionnaires are filled out in isolation, students do not have the opportunity to discuss and come up with suggestions for improvement

Using an Electronic Meeting the students were able to share their comments, add to them and develop each others ideas. Giving anonymity to the students was an essential aspect of the evaluation. The simultaneous input of ideas makes this interchange economic time-wise.

Lynch and Wood report that "it is a requirement of University policy that students are informed on the outcomes of the evaluations, and what the lecturer intends to do about any shortcomings or ideas for improvement". Use of Electronic Meetings allows the lecturers to give immediate feedback to those students who participated in the evaluation.

To improve feedback and learning, students in some subjects were asked to list what they had gained from the subject. To explore learning styles volunteer students were asked questions such as:

• what techniques do you use to understand a topic?
• what have you learnt about learning this semester?
• if you have a problem in understanding, what do you do?

Many valuable comments and suggestions were received, not only about course content but about administration issues, feedback that was "far superior to that gathered by any other method".

Electronic Meetings in schools

Bob Briggs of the University of Arizona and Howard Brown of the Anacostia High School in Washington DC have used Electronic Meeting technology to make an exciting contribution to a local school. The techniques that are revolutionizing meetings in industry may well create a similar revolution in the classroom. Students, to the consternation of some teachers, can even be asked what they want to learn.

In one of the first sessions fifth grade students were asked what subjects they thought were important:

• If you could learn anything you like, what would it be?
• What do you have the most fun making?
• Who is your most favorite famous person and why?
• What do you have the most fun doing?

Student responses to these questions helped frame projects and problems throughout the remainder of the study.

To make an exercise of writing letters more relevant the pupils voted electronically to choose their favorite living person. They used the Electronic Meeting technology to collectively structure their ideas for a letter to the winner, Michael Jordan, asking him to visit the school. In fact Michael Jordan did not visit but subsequent efforts did get visits from a general in the Marine Corps and from an astronaut.

A history related project developed great enthusiasm in the teeth of initial vocal feed back from the students that "history is boring". An anonymous electronic discussion on the subject revealed that the students wanted "to make history, not study it". The students collectively wrote a book on the concept of greatness that they sent to major figures such as the President and the Poet Laureate asking for feedback. The students voted electronically to decide who was their favorite person from history and then extended the discussion by defining the attributes of greatness in priority sequence. The top three attributes were 'hard work', 'leadership' and 'inspiring'.

The students also used the equipment to create a poem about Martin Luther King.

There were inevitably occasions when the students took advantage of anonymity to indulge in 'flaming' i.e. entering offensive remarks. This was almost always associated with the students getting bored with a subject or how it was being presented.

In terms of student achievement there were measurable improvements in their writing, as shown by grammatical analysis of written artifacts, and other specific improvements and benefits.

At a school in Tucson, the Palo Verde Magnet High School, Mary Lonsdale has used Electronic Meetings technology. In a comprehensive level English class electronic discussion supported literature analysis including characters, setting and the plot, and style analysis, including metaphors, similes, symbolism and imagery. Among other activities, students wrote a novelette, first brainstorming the characters and settings and then co-operatively developing the chapters.

Electronic Meeting technology seems to generate innovative ideas in education as elsewhere. Melissa Sue Glynn and Jeannette Quintana of the University of Arizona have worked with Debra Cunningham & Dr. Sam Cooper of Cholla Magnet High School in Tucson to incorporate mock trials and jury deliberations into a sophomore English class using Electronic Meeting technology. Two sets of student jurors were selected as part of the mock trial. The first set of jurors used an Electronic Meeting and the second deliberated in the traditional face-to-face method. "Preliminary results indicate that the deliberations held with GSS encouraged critical thinking, communication, and equal participation with students."

Summary:

Electronic Meetings can improve the effectiveness of adult training by providing instant and accurate feedback to keep the training on track and ensure that the priority issues are always addressed.

As one would expect Electronic Meetings are becoming regular features in business schools.

In school education the contribution of Electronic Meetings is innovative and measurable.

Let us now consider the application of Electronic Meetings where we would expect them to be used to good effect, namely the IT Department.

Chapter 10

THE IT DEPARTMENT

Electronic Meetings make it possible for IT Departments to speed up the design and implementation of solutions, whilst at the same time keeping in closer contact with customers.

JAD (Joint Application Development)

Electronic Meetings make JAD sessions quicker and more productive (JAD is an acronym for Joint Application Development, a well-established process whereby IT people and their customers jointly design new computer systems). In general JAD sessions are used to:

- gather user requirements
- analyze these requirements
- design user interfaces.

Dick Orth of IBM has run many JAD sessions with Electronic Meetings. As part of a JAD, he runs sessions to define the business requirements for a product or a service. High-level steps can include:

1. define the current environment
2. identify the problems with this environment
3. prioritize the problems
4. identify the characteristics and benefits of the 'perfect' environment
5. prioritize the benefits and map back to the problems
6. identify how you know when you have received each benefit.

The facilitators in the Consultancy arm of the NatWest Bank in the UK have run many JAD sessions using Electronic Meeting technology. Ade Coker, one of their experienced facilitators, has found Electronic Meetings particularly effective in situations of a difficult political or personally sensitive nature.

In another example of a joint meeting with users, an Australian Government Department in Canberra ran an Electronic Meeting so that a group of senior managers could explore the best way to utilize a new statistical system that was about to be launched. The system had taken several years and millions of dollars to produce, and the participants at the meeting had already received a typical range of briefing literature and process reports.

When allowed to make anonymous comments on the proposed new system the participants revealed that they were barely aware of its existence. This was a real shock to the developers who were fortunately then able to use capabilities of the Electronic Meeting, facilitated by John Richards of GroupWare Australia, to repair the communication gap.

Software quality

A very effective way to improve the quality of software is to use *Fagan* inspections. A Fagan inspection is a structured review intended to detect defects in software development documents and in code. Such inspections have been carried out by software engineers around the world for more than twenty years, hence there is existing information about the effectiveness of these inspections when run conventionally, i.e. without the use of Electronic Meeting technology. These statistics can thus be compared with the results achieved using Electronic Meetings.

Michiel van Genuchten of Simac, Wieger Cornelissen of Philips Medical Systems and Cor van Dijk of Baan Company have measured the results from Fagan inspections using Electronic Meeting technology. They conclude, "the effectiveness of the EMS supported inspections is considerably higher (than traditional inspections)". Measures have been made of the *efficiency* and *effectiveness* of logging defects, both before the meeting and during the meeting. The Fagan process distinguishes between *major* and *minor* defects, hence there are eight possible measures, and on all of them Electronic Meetings show significantly improved performance, with an improvement by a factor greater than ten on three of the eight measures.

This work shows that Electronic Meetings can improve the quality of software. The techniques for finding and recording the number of errors can be applied in many other Quality programs.

Process modelling

A variety of different techniques are being successfully used to combine the capabilities of Electronic Meetings with computerized modeling to illustrate how a business process works at present and how the improved version will work.

IDEF

IDEF is a modeling process developed initially for the U.S. Air Force. IDEF0 (pronounced eye deaf zero) is a logical method for describing complex business processes, a process being defined as a group of activities that together produce an output. IDEF0 uses a technique called '*functional decomposition*' to break a process into its constituent parts.

Douglas Dean and James Lee of the University of Arizona have considerable experience of using IDEF modeling in conjunction with Electronic Meeting technology. They have found the capability of involving more participants than can be accommodated in a conventional meeting to be very helpful, in that all the key experts can work together to produce the model. This avoids extensive post-meeting reviews and model revision. The semantic checking built into IDEF0 is very helpful in making modeling sessions more effective. The combination of such features results in the time required to develop a model in an Electronic Meeting being typically half that required using conventional approaches.

Amsterdam CID

Gert-Jan de Vreede and Henk Sol of the Delft University of Technology used Electronic Meetings to help develop an information system for the Amsterdam Municipal Police Force Criminal Investigation Department. It is estimated that organized crime has worldwide profits of 1 trillion US dollars, almost as much as the U.S. annual federal budget. There are approximately 600 criminal organizations in Holland alone. In order to optimize the effectiveness of the Police in this complex area, a different type of information system was needed.

The design of such a system (called ACOST, Atlas of Criminal Organisations and Societal Trends) necessitated extensive contact with potential users. Participants included representatives not only from the Amsterdam Police Force, but also from the Mayor of Amsterdam and the judicial authorities. Electronic Meetings were applied in the following areas:

- specification of user requirements
- specification and evaluation of prototypes
- data collection (data on organized crime was "very efficiently collected" by this process)
- user instruction
- simulation of work procedures.

In order to more closely model the Amsterdam CID processes, de Vreede and his colleagues used animated simulation. By watching an animated cartoon-like model on a computer screen, users are more easily and quickly able to relate to the model and point out errors and omissions. de Vreede ran sessions using static and dynamic modeling in parallel with Electronic Meeting technology to collect comments, queries and suggestions for improvement. Feedback from the participants was very good, with the questions 'Is an Electronic Meeting more productive than an manual meeting?' and 'Did you find the Electronic Meeting technology user friendly?' receiving average responses of 4.7 out of 5.

The use of Electronic Meetings was a critical success factor for the project. The designers commented:

"We are convinced that it would be very hard (in time and money) to get a qualitatively better set of user requirements, especially given the relatively short time period involved."

And a comment from a user:

"ACOST is a system that we built together. It's something we should be proud of and proud to present to others."

Which is surely what it is all about. If only all users felt the same about their computer systems!

Skill definition

Skill definition in IT Departments is a vital issue, particularly with the rate of changes in technology. New skills have to be developed quickly and it can be genuinely difficult to define and recognize a skill level in the new areas of computing.

Tammy Lowry and colleagues in Texaco used Electronic Meetings extensively to define skill based job descriptions and job families covering 2,000 IT employees in nine locations and seven different business units. The process included:

- meeting with seven representative teams to create lists of competencies (a competency being defined as a grouping of a unique set of skills)
- consolidating the seven lists into one list
- reviewing and validating the list with management
- creating a team for each competency
- meeting with each team to create a list of skill bands and behaviors (a band is defined as a level of proficiency within a skill, a behavior demonstrates the skill at that band)
- reviewing and validating results from competency teams with participants and management groups.

Assessing the effectiveness of IT systems

An established way of assess the effectiveness of IT systems is to make comparisons with other organizations. However, it is not easy to make such comparisons quickly and cheaply. For ten medical institutions, Electronic Meetings provided the solution. Consultant JR Holt ran a series of ten meetings at the end of which the institutions were able to make a detailed assessment of their systems by two criteria, effectiveness and market need. The meetings lasted 2 – 4 hours, with 10 – 30 participants, typically members of the Board of Directors, Chief Medical Officers, Chief Physicians and Surgeons and Departmental Heads. Seventy-three different IT systems were covered. The end result was data for the Chief Information Officers that exceeded their expectations, with strong support for repeating the exercise the following year.

Summary:

Electronic Meetings are being used to support solution development in key areas of IT Departments including JAD, software quality assurance, process modeling and skills analysis.

The potential is unlimited.

Where next in the book

The last eight chapters have presented a wide range of examples of Electronic Meetings in actual use. The intention is that readers will have

- seen one or many applications that are worth following up personally
- begun to develop a conviction that Electronic Meetings are an essential tool for any significant organization.

Readers who want to get into more detail about how to plan Electronic Meetings should continue with the next four chapters.

Readers who want immediate action may like to go to Chapter 15, *Running Electronic Meetings*.

Readers wanting a more strategic view of the effect of Electronic Meetings on the organization may like to skip to Chapter 16, *Implementing Electronic Meetings across the organization*.

PLANNING
ELECTRONIC MEETINGS

Chapter 11

EXCHANGING INFORMATION AND OPINIONS

The previous eight chapters give many real examples of the use of Electronic Meetings in a wide variety of situations. In the next four chapters we will look more closely at how typical Electronic Meetings are planned and run. As introduced in Chapter 2, one approach is to see a meeting as consisting of four basic activities, illustrated in figure 11.1:

- talk about the subject, contributing facts and opinions - *exchange information and opinions.*
- input ideas or proposals as to what should be done - *develop proposals for action.*
- consider the pros and cons of the proposed actions - *evaluate ideas and solutions.*
- decide what should have priority and then agree who will do what - *vote on priorities and get commitment.*

Figure 11.1 - Typical sessions of Electronic Meetings

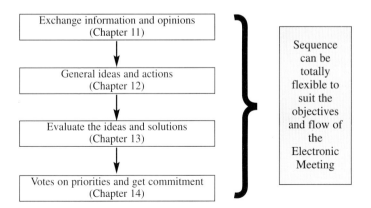

Exchange information and opinions
(Chapter 11)

General ideas and actions
(Chapter 12)

Evaluate the ideas and solutions
(Chapter 13)

Votes on priorities and get commitment
(Chapter 14)

Sequence can be totally flexible to suit the objectives and flow of the Electronic Meeting

The chairperson and participants can run such activities as often as needed, in any sequence and with many variations. There are of course other types of sessions in Electronic Meetings, for example graphical simulation for business process modeling or special techniques to stimulate creativity.

But before defining the agenda, we need to decide what we want out of the meeting.

Defining the objectives and the deliverables

'Deliverables' are an important concept for Electronic Meetings, and are more specific than 'objectives'. For example, if an objective is to discuss an issue, then the deliverable for this objective might be a printout showing the arguments for and against the issue, with the results of any votes that were taken.

The deliverables give a measure of the objectives of a meeting with a precision that has not previously been practical. This is a fundamental breakthrough from Electronic Meetings.

Once the objectives and deliverables are specified, the agenda can be prepared as a list of activities such as are shown in Figure 11.1. This process of preparing the agenda for an Electronic Meeting is a very useful exercise because it necessitates a clear analysis of how the meeting is intended to achieve its objectives.

Most meetings include at least one session of *exchanging information and opinions*, which is the subject of this chapter. This requires that a set of issues, questions or headings be defined to focus the discussion.

Defining the issues for discussion

A session to *exchange information and opinions* could be held for example to:

* share information on the background to a problem or situation
* ask for feedback from a group of people such as customers, employees or a review board

This type of electronic discussion is sometimes termed a 'shared thinking' environment. It is a powerful technique for summarizing the knowledge and opinions of a group of people. These people do not of course need to be in the same room or even on the same continent.

An example of pre-set questions is given in Figure 11.2, showing a set of questions about a proposed new service.

Figure 11.2 - Opinion feedback session - possible questions

After a description of this proposed new service, the participants select from the questions shown in Figure 11.2 and enter their free format reply into a window such as that illustrated in Figure 11.3. The participants type their input into the lower box, have the computer check the spelling if required and then use a key or the mouse to transmit it. Since the input is usually anonymous, participants can actually make comments on any subject they wish, even to suggest a coffee break.

Figure 11.3 - Opinion feedback session - comment entry window

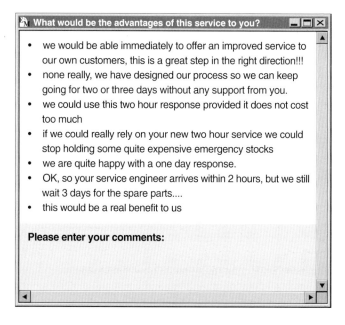

Figure 11.3 illustrates participants entering their comments while seeing what the other participants have contributed. If on the other hand participants do not see what the others have entered, they can only give their own original opinions.

When participants see others' input the discussion is likely to be richer and more complete because ideas can be bounced around between participants. Input will also be quicker because participants can enter 'I agree with...' or 'I do not agree with...' (of particular value to those who are not keen typists). A build-up of common opinions can take place and this helps summary of the input at a later stage. It is of course quite possible to take both options:

1. start by asking participants to give their input without seeing other participants' input
2. let participants see each others' input
3. have a second session so that participants can enter any new or modified input.

While participants are giving their input the facilitator or chairperson should be monitoring input for clarity and might for example ask for further elaboration of the last comment in Figure 11.3 ('this would be a real benefit to us'). This comment is of limited value since it is not specific about the benefit. The participant in question can remain anonymous and type in further information as he or she wishes. Alternatively the participant could expand on the comment verbally, since there may be no great secret about it. The facilitator might then ask the participant to type in the reply so as to put it on the record.

In most meetings the full list of replies or comments on any question will more than fill one window so participants simply scroll up and down to display any particular section.

Some Electronic Meetings have very simple sets of questions. For example in discussing a situation that needs improvement:

- what are the problems?
- what is working well?
- what has already been tried?

As another example, a reasonable set of questions after any event might be:

- what went right?
- what went wrong?

- what should we change?
- what should we not change?
- any other comments or suggestions?

Questions such as 'what should we not change/what works well?' can have a useful stabilizing effect. It is easy at times put too much emphasis on 'what are we doing wrong/what can be improved?' As the number of participants in the meeting increase there is a growing possibility that almost every aspect of the subject under discussion will be criticized by someone. Hence it is good to allow participants to identify the positive as well as the negative.

Electronic Meetings to exchange information can be short and small. An Electronic Meeting that one of the authors set up a few years ago concerned a project that was taking longer to plan than it should have done. The following simple questions were put to the five participants:

- who owns this project?
- who initiated it?
- what are its objectives?
- when is it due to be completed?

From the five participants there were four anonymous replies of "I do" to the first question. The meeting collapsed in laughter and a situation that was beginning to involve some tedious and time consuming internal politics was resolved in about 15 minutes in the greatest good humor - thanks to a short Electronic Meeting.

Questions can of course be more imaginative. For example, at the start of a meeting, a question such as:

'What do you think the other departments want from this meeting?'

can increase understanding between people from different departments or organizations.

It is not necessary to give all the questions to the participants at one time. As was shown with a real example in Chapter 8 concerning skills management, the questions can be given one after the other, with participants reading the responses to one question before proceeding to the next. There is no golden rule for choosing between these approaches; it is a matter of judgment for chairperson and facilitator.

It is important to define questions such as the above carefully. For example, the participants could be invited to discuss any aspect of a project or restricted to a specific aspect, such as how to improve its implementation. If the issues are complex or contentious it is sometimes valuable to test the wording on people who are not directly involved in planning the meeting.

Using anonymity effectively

All of the input shown in Figure 11.3 is anonymous, that is to say there is no indication who made the comments, or whether one person has made several comments and others none. However, anonymity can be switched on or off during the meeting. Participants know when anonymity is switched off because they are asked to type in their name or an identification such as 'small customer', 'large customer', 'accounts', or 'marketing'.

When group identification is used the window might look as in Figure 11.4, where each entry has the participant's group automatically attached to it by the software. In this example, the customers have signed in as 'small customer' or 'large customer'. Within these groups no one knows which individual customer makes any particular comment.

To pursue the example further, it might appear from inspection of the input in Figure 11.4 that the large customers are more interested in the new service than the small customers. The facilitator might pick this up, and add another question or set up a vote to see if this is indeed the case. It might then be useful to ask the small customers what could be done to make the proposed new service of more interest to them.

Anonymity should be used as appropriate – at times it is valuable to encourage an uninhibited flow of ideas and comments while at other times it is important to know who said what.

Figure 11.4 - Opinion feedback session - participants' comments with group identification

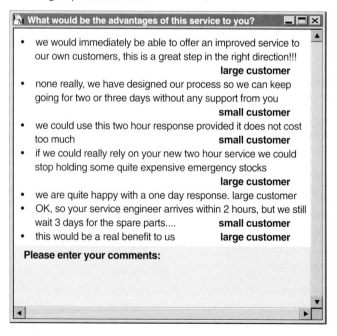

Summarizing the input

When the participants have produced their comments and opinions, the chairperson or facilitator might ask the participants to help in summarizing their input. The input would be displayed on the large screen and also on each participant's screen. After suitable discussion, comments might be merged or categorized. Merging joins similar comments and ideas together, while categorizing puts the comments and ideas into categories such as departments, people, time scales, document sections or key issues. In this way no input is lost or ignored.

Suitable categories could be suggested either by the chairperson or by the participants, maybe picking up comments that stand out as encapsulating important points. For example, suitable categories for one of the questions in Figure 11.2, 'do you have any comments on our current services?' might be:

* pricing
* contracts
* invoicing
* week-end support
* response times
* training of service engineers

Categorization could go into further detail. For instance the last category 'training of service engineers' could be further divided into:

* servicing existing products
* knowledge of new products
* knowledge of contracts and pricing policies.

Multiple copies of comments can be made if they belong in more than one category. For example the comment 'I would like to see the service engineers better trained and available at week-ends' could be put into two different categories.

Disagreement between participants does not necessarily need to be resolved. If Marketing thinks the price is too high and Finance think it is too low, we may be able to accept this difference for the time being and move on.

In some situations, simply identifying differences of opinion can be very useful. A customer who sees that no one else wants a certain feature on the product might be more understanding that it is not available. An employee who sees that no one else is bothered by the new office layout might attach less importance to the issue.

In any subsequent meeting on the same subject all the comments from this meeting are available, so there is no needless repetition and no misunderstanding about what was previously discussed and agreed.

Agenda for a customer feedback meeting

Many organizations get value from discussing new products and services with their customers. Electronic Meetings are an excellent way of doing this, as illustrated in Chapter 3. Figure 11.5 shows a possible for a customer feedback meeting, with possible times in minutes.

Figure 11.5 - Possible agenda of a customer feedback meeting

Welcome/objectives of meeting	10mins.
Description of the proposed new service	as req'd
Introduction to Electronic Meetings and icebreaker	10
Electronic sign-in by participants	10
Participants respond to prepared questions	20 - 40
Participants' read all input, give further response	20
Agree summary of the participants' input	30
Vote to prioritize issues (if appropriate) and discuss	as req'd
Printout for participants (options)	
Survey of participants' opinions of the meeting	10

The introduction to Electronic Meetings should be no longer than five or ten minutes since participants learn best about the system by using it. As discussed in Chapter 2, it might well be appropriate in this type of meeting for representatives of the 'home team' to contribute to the meeting by answering questions and asking for interpretation when appropriate.

On-line participants' survey

It is good practice at the end of an Electronic Meeting to ask the participants to complete an anonymous survey to find out how satisfied they are with the meeting. The survey usually includes questions designed to provide a numeric measure of the perceived value of the meeting in addition to open-ended questions inviting comments and suggestions, as illustrated in Figure 11.6.

Figure 11.6 - Participant satisfaction survey

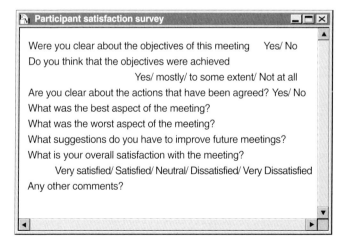

A simple participant survey as shown in Figure 11.6 would take about ten minutes and the results would be immediately shared among all participants as the final session of the meeting (unless the chairperson and facilitator were particularly cowardly!). A follow-up survey at a later date could establish whether the meeting really did deliver results.

Summary:

Electronic Meetings are ideal for frankly and honestly exchanging information and opinions on any subject. The chairperson and/or facilitator set up initial questions or headings in order to focus discussion. These can be changed or added to quickly and easily.

Anonymity allows participants to express all their ideas, even if not fully thought out or politically risky. Input is often merged or summarized into categories without losing any of the content. When appropriate, participants can give their input at different times, or from different locations.

An 'exchange of information and opinions' session can take as little as five minutes or can occupy the entire meeting.

After we have exchanged information and opinions the next stage is usually to build on that input by generating ideas, tasks, risks, actions or whatever is appropriate to the meeting. This is the subject of the next chapter.

Chapter 12

GENERATING IDEAS AND ACTIONS

This chapter describes how participants generate a list of ideas in a session of an Electronic Meeting. The ideas could be whatever is appropriate for the meeting including:

- tasks
- key issues
- problems
- symptoms
- risks
- questions.

We assume that information and opinions on the subject have already been shared, the structure of the meeting being illustrated in Figure 12.1.

Figure 12.1 - Basic sessions of Electronic Meetings

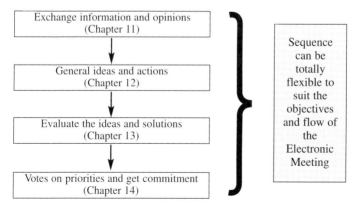

Electronic Meetings are an excellent tool for generating alternative ideas, rather than accepting the first idea that comes up. Taking the first idea may save time in the short term but the first idea may not be the best. A further advantage of Electronic Meetings in developing ideas and proposals is that the ease of managing them provides the opportunity to develop several alternatives to some depth, maybe with groups of participants working in parallel. If we can work in detail on several alternatives and then combine the best features of each alternative, we are likely to end up with a much better solution.

In developing ideas in an Electronic Meeting one can:

- produce *a short list of ideas*, perhaps one or two per participant
- generate *a free wheeling long list of ideas*, everything that the participants can think of
- use *creativity techniques* to develop new and innovative ideas.

The choice between these approaches depends on the subject and deliverables of the session, and also on the culture of the participants. Parallel entry of ideas makes these sessions quick and productive.

A short list of ideas

In some meetings the participants have ideas or proposals in mind before the discussion even starts. Maybe there are only a few options available and the objective of the meeting is to identify the option that has the most common support and then improve it as far as possible.

Let us suppose we are receiving feedback from customers that is critical of one of our service offerings, let us say Service X, and we therefore need to improve it. The participants at the meeting include people from the relevant departments plus customers and key suppliers, some of whom are not physically present in the meeting room but are participating remotely.

After discussion of the symptoms and environment of the problem, as described in the previous chapter, participants might receive on their screens a question such as:

'What are your ideas to improve Service X?'

When a shortlist is required, the chairperson or facilitator asks participants to submit their top priority idea first. This makes the session easier to manage and avoids subsequent duplication in that participants do not need to repeat ideas already submitted.

Participants submit ideas as illustrated in Figure 12.2. If the ideas are complex, participants can submit a short title, adding further description as comments on this title.

Similar ideas can be merged together. For example, in Figure 12.2 there is commonality between the ideas for the help desk, for better documentation and for training the customers' people.

Figure 12.2 - Ideas to improve Service X

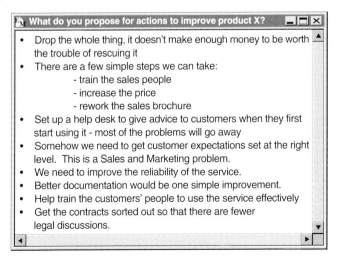

Anonymity has been useful because it has allowed participants to make proposals that they may not want to make openly, perhaps for political reasons or because their proposals are not fully thought through. The session becomes a team exercise to produce the best list of proposals, not a competition to be seen to make the best proposal or an endurance test to defend one's own proposals to the bitter end. At all times there is full and free verbal discussion.

A long list of ideas

Quite often the meeting owner and participants want to develop a long list of ideas to be sure that all the angles of the subject are covered and no potentially good idea is overlooked. Electronic Meetings are absolutely ideal for this. It is a very natural process for participants in an Electronic Meeting to continue to enter their ideas until they are exhausted, producing ideas at a rate of perhaps one per minute per participant.

A long list of ideas can be reduced to manageable proportions by merging ideas, voting to choose the most important or by categorizing them. Categorization in this context would mean for example assigning tasks to people or to departments, organizing subjects into sections of a document or allocating time scales to activities.

Creativity techniques

Creative approaches to problems and opportunities are important in a rapidly changing world. Many techniques have been developed that encourage and even force a creative approach, rather than simply asking people to write down a list of ideas as discussed immediately above. Brainstorming is one well-established creativity technique.

In brainstorming participants are invited to produce large numbers of ideas, particularly ideas that may be initially incomplete, unrealistic or even outrageous. The quantity of ideas is the first measure of success, regardless of the apparent quality or realism of the ideas. The hope, often realized in practice, is that practical new solutions will emerge by developing and combining the brainstormed ideas, solutions that the individuals could not have developed by themselves in their own office - or even in their bath!

Electronic Meetings are ideal for this brainstorming process because:

- all contributions are stored, so nothing is lost
- anonymity encourages imagination and creativity
- details can easily be added to ideas
- participants can easily see all the ideas.

A particular technique that can be used during Electronic Brainstorming is that each new idea, is sent at random to another participant. The receiving participant can then add their own idea and the combined ideas are sent to another participant, again at random. This random exchange of input has been shown to generate more ideas than conventional brainstorming.

Robert Briggs of the University of Arizona and Daniel Mittleman of DePaul University have used this random distribution of ideas in Electronic Meetings for what they term 'directed brainstorming'. For example, if the objective of the session is to develop ideas for cost reduction, participants would enter one idea and then see on their screen an idea that had been entered by someone else. The Meeting Owner could then challenge the participants to combine or to improve the ideas in front of them. Further cycles could introduce different variations.

There are a number of ways of structuring this process and it has shown to be an excellent way of developing creative ideas and solutions.

Other established techniques for developing creativity include the use of word lists or pictures to force development of ideas.

To some people the random and unstructured nature of a creative brainstorming session may appear unsatisfactory. Nevertheless, many people have experience of creative brainstorming to produce large numbers of ideas and hence better solutions.

Summary:

There are different techniques for generating lots of ideas in Electronic Meetings. Some situations require a short list of specific proposals, some a long list of ideas and some the use of creativity techniques.

This type of session can be used to develop any lists of items, such as actions, risks, tasks, subjects or key issues.

Electronic Meetings are excellent for idea creation, since all ideas are recorded, anonymity increases creativity, remote participants can conveniently give their input and the parallel entry of data reduces the time required.

Having produced a list of ideas and potential solutions, a good next step would be to ask the participants to comment on them and evaluate them. How to do this quickly and effectively is described in the next chapter.

Chapter 13

EVALUATING IDEAS AND SOLUTIONS

When a list of ideas or solutions has been developed it can be beneficial to step back and discuss them before decisions are taken. Electronic Meetings make it simple, quick and easy for participants to explore even a long list of ideas and record their objective comments.

It is easy to include remote participants for this stage of an Electronic Meeting. External experts or other interested parties can be invited to contribute their comments via their PC from anywhere in the world.

A distinction between generating ideas and evaluating them is one of the many reasons for the success of Electronic Meetings. In conventional meetings, these two functions are often inextricably mixed and confused.

Recording objective comments about each idea has specific advantages:

- it ensures that there is agreement on the meaning
- it ensures that participants are aware of all relevant factors in subsequent voting and decision sessions
- it acts as an audit trail to support subsequent decisions
- it will be possible to learn from the current discussion when similar issues arise in the future
- participants can identify the positive features of each idea.

If the participants already agree on the advantages and disadvantages of each idea then this session will be short. Figure 13.1 shows how this session can fit in with other sessions in an Electronic Meeting.

Figure 13.1 - Typical sessions of Electronic Meetings

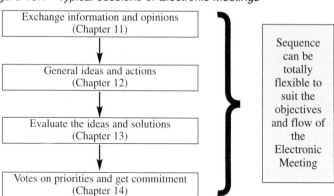

A typical window that the participants might see is illustrated in Figure 13.2.

Figure 13.2 Evaluating a list of solutions.

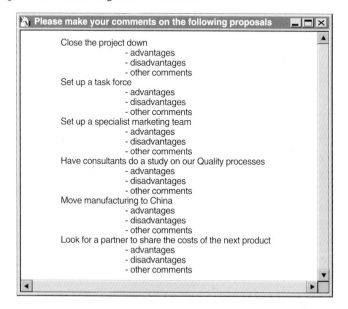

In Figure 13.2 the participants are asked to record the advantages, the disadvantages and any other comments on each of six proposals that have been produced. To do this they select a line from Figure 13.2 and they will then see a window as illustrated in Figure 13.3. While making their input, the participants usually see the other participants' input to avoid repetition, though as described in Chapter 11, these sessions can start with the participants not seeing each others' input so that that they are able to give their own ideas without being influenced by others. The participants then review all the comments to see whether they want to make any additions or modifications. Differences in opinion can be further explored using Electronic Voting, as described in the next chapter.

Figure 13.3 Entering a comment on a proposed solution.

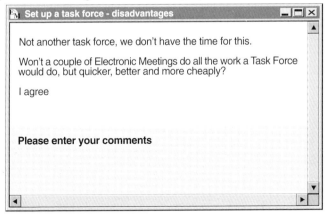

One frequent extension of the headings shown in Figure 13.2 is to add other levels to the hierarchy so that participants are asked to comment on advantages and disadvantages of each solution under detailed headings such as financial, environmental, market share, etc. When the issues are sufficiently important, this is an excellent way of developing a detailed and very focused discussion.

It is important to have a positive frame of mind when discussing and evaluating ideas. Based on their experience with Synectics, John Ceserani and Peter Greatwood have described a technique for 'open-minded constructive evaluation' of ideas in which the discussion of an idea starts by listing three positive features. This simple discipline helps identify the best features of ideas with a view to combining and improving them.

Another way to stimulate a range of viewpoints is for the participants to adopt roles from Edward de Bono's book, *'Six Thinking Hats'*. de Bono's colored hats reflect different viewpoints, for example being critical, emotive, neutral or optimistic and have been used to good effect in Electronic Meetings.

A specific example of using an Electronic Meeting to discuss and get commitment on new proposals was a meeting in a pharmaceutical company run with facilitation support from Jon Matthews of Ventana UK. At this meeting the project manager described a proposed new business process to 15 people representing the worldwide operations of the company. During the project manager's 140-minute presentation, the 15 participants recorded their comments and questions on their PC's. Hence the speaker was not interrupted, except for urgent questions.

At the end of the project manager's presentation all the comments and questions, 351 of them, were collected electronically and reviewed by the participants. The comments were divided into:

- issues to be addressed
- comments
- suggestions
- benefits.

After discussion it became clear that the most significant area of concern was the introduction and start up of the system. Eighty-four issues were identified for improving this critical part of the project.

It is useful to consider what might have happened without the Electronic Meeting facilities. There are a number of alternatives:

1. After the 140-minute presentation the participants would have had little time for discussion and might have accepted the proposed system as described by the Project Manager. Implementation would have proceeded without the improvements resulting from the 84 issues.
2. The participants might have rejected the proposed system. They would have given the Project Manager a few reasons that might have been summarized on a flip chart or two. With only this incomplete feedback the Project Manager would not be clear what changes were needed.
3. The participants might have interrupted the Project Manager on average every 24 seconds with their comments or questions and the presentation would have collapsed.

Many readers will have seen all three of these unsatisfactory outcomes at different meetings.

If the above numbers are representative, there is an enormous wastage of good ideas in conventional meetings. This example may also help explain why people sometimes do not commit as fully to their proposals as managers would wish: the reason is that people have too many unanswered questions and suppressed ideas for improvement. Managers need more Electronic Meetings to get their people committed!

The freedom to make anonymous comments is important when evaluating ideas. Some classical experiments carried out by

Solomon Asch in the early 1950's showed how difficult it is for people to express open dissent in a meeting and the extent to which people are influenced by the group of which they are a part. Asch submitted students to a safe, non-stressful experiment in which they were asked to make an easy judgment about the length of a line drawn on a card. The students had to say which of three lines, of clearly different lengths, was the same length as the line on the card. The research issue was to investigate to what extent the subjects of the experiments would be swayed by wrong answers given by their peers. Although he or she was unaware of it, only one person in each group was actually being experimented on, the others having been primed to give wrong answers when so instructed. Somewhat disconcertingly, over many experiments, some 30% of the students followed the majority and gave wrong answers, against the clear evidence of their eyes.

If in the stress free environment of a student experiment, on the absolutely factual issue of the length of a line, people were unwilling to disagree with their peers, then the anonymity feature of Electronic Meetings has a real value in enabling open discussion, leading to better business solutions.

For a real life example of the antithesis of the open discussion in an Electronic Meeting, Irving Janis has coined the word Groupthink. A well-recorded situation where Electronic Meetings would doubtless have been of great value (but were unfortunately not available) was the unsuccessful Bay of Pigs invasion of Cuba carried out during the Kennedy presidency. Many people have published their versions of the event and Janis has analyzed in detail the key meetings and conversations. There were no improper activities to blame, it just happened that the uncertainties about the objectives of the invasion and the considerable doubts about its implementation were not fully evaluated in a Presidential meeting. No one wanted to risk "losing the approval of fellow members of their primary work group", a concern that inhibits many people from asking direct questions or voicing their doubts. Yet if the issues are important and the doubts valid, failure to discuss them may lead to less than optimum decisions and solutions.

Summary

Summarizing the arguments for and against proposals before voting on them ensures that the votes, and the ensuing business solutions, are soundly based. Electronic Meetings make this process quick and effective.

Remote participants can make valuable contributions at this stage of a meeting.

A set of considered proposals might be the deliverable of the meeting, in which case the meeting can now close. However, many meetings will carry on to vote on these proposals and commit to actions, as described in the next chapter.

Chapter 14

VOTES, DECISIONS AND COMMITMENTS

Voting in Electronic Meetings fundamentally improves how people come to decisions and commit to implement solutions. Figure 14.1 illustrates how voting can fit in the logical flow of an Electronic Meeting.

Figure 14.1 - Typical sessions of Electronic Meetings

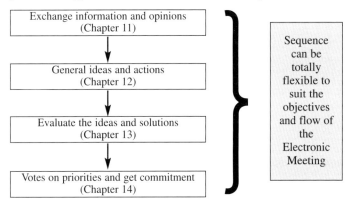

In conventional meetings votes are usually taken at the end of a discussion to confirm agreement. In Electronic Meetings voting is also used throughout the meeting to achieve something unachievable in a conventional meeting, that is to identify continuously and rigorously the important issues for discussion. Hence no time is wasted on issues:

• that are not important
• where the participants are already agreed (but may not otherwise realize it until after a lengthy discussion).

As discussed in Chapter 2, the wide use of voting in Electronic Meetings does not imply dependence on majority decision where this is not appropriate. In many circumstances one person will actually take a decision after an issue has been fully explored in an Electronic Meeting.

However, when the participants in a meeting are at a senior level or if they represent different functions or organizations it is highly beneficial if agreement can be reached, whoever is nominally taking the decision. If agreement cannot be reached, it is important that the discussion has been clear and honest. People can support a decision they did not initially agree with if they have been able to put their own views forward for fair consideration and if they are clear about the reasons for the decision. In these situations Electronic Voting has unique and far-reaching benefits.

Public, show-of-hands voting is appropriate at times in an Electronic Meeting to formalize agreement. Anonymous voting allows issues to be fully explored, but clearly is not used to the extent of avoiding personal responsibility for decisions. Let us first look briefly at voting in a conventional meeting.

Voting in a conventional meeting

In a conventional meeting voting is usually restricted. When a list of proposals is being voted on, participants usually have to choose just one proposal from the list. It is tacitly assumed in a conventional meeting that all the participants will fully commit to the proposal that receives the most votes.

However, a simple 'hands up all those in favor' vote in a conventional meeting can lead to opinions being suppressed and wrong decisions being taken.

It is easy to show how conventional meetings take wrong decisions. Suppose we have a meeting where twelve people are to vote for one of five proposals. If the votes are as shown in Figure 14.2 then proposal A is the winner without question. However, participants in an Electronic Meeting could come to a different and better decision by rating the five proposals with more precision, as will be seen in the next section.

Figure 14.2 - Possible vote at a conventional meeting

Proposal A	5 votes
Proposal B	3 votes
Proposal C	2 votes
Proposal D	2 votes
Proposal E	0 votes

Analyzing the vote spread

Using one format of Electronic Vote, participants can rate the five proposals in Figure 14.2 on a scale of 1 - 10. Participants can read on their PC the advantages and disadvantages of each proposal and then enter a number between 1 and 10. There must be agreement on the meaning of the scale, for example 10 as 'excellent, must do', 5 as 'OK I can live with it', 1 as 'this would be a disaster'.

Suppose we have the same 12 people as at the conventional meeting above, voting again on the five proposals A, B, C, D and E, on our scale of 1 - 10. As soon as the vote is complete the proposals are listed in priority order on everyone's screen, as illustrated in Figures 14.3 and 14.4.

The bar chart, or histogram, shown in Figure 14.3 is extremely valuable for getting a quick picture of the results of the vote. The table in Figure 14.4 is the working data from which the chairperson and participants can decide if the pattern of votes shows sufficient commitment and identify precisely which issues require further discussion.

In Figure 14.3, B is the preferred proposal and A is actually the fourth choice of the five proposals. Yet each participant made their first choice according to their vote in a conventional meeting, as shown in Figure 14.2! So how can we have such a different result?

Figure 14.3 Rating of proposals A, B, C, D, E

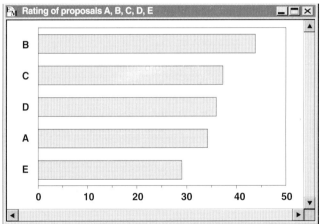

The explanation for this result is that although five people do indeed think A is an excellent proposal, there are five people who think A would be a disaster. In contrast, proposal B, although rated excellent by only three people, is highly rated by another two people, acceptable to another six and rated as disastrous by no one. In some circumstances therefore B could be the best choice because it has solid support from 10 of the 12 participants. Proposal A, although chosen by a conventional vote, is not the best choice if it matters that almost half the participants in the meeting consider that it would be a disaster (and it might not matter). Figure 14.4 shows the possible votes of the meeting participants.

Figure 14.4 - Rating votes for proposals A, B, C, D, E.

Rating votes for proposals A, B, C, D, E.										
	10	**9**	**8**	**7**	**6**	**5**	**4**	**3**	**2**	**1**	**Total**
A	5					1		1		5	63
B	3	2	0			6		1			81
C	2	2				6		2			71
D	2		1		1	4		3		1	64
E	0		2			6		2		2	54

It would appear from the spread of votes in Figure 14.4 that the meeting is not yet at a consensus, since a quick inspection shows that the participants' opinions are widely divergent. However, if we are selecting the one best proposal, we can decide immediately that we don't need to spend any more time discussing proposals D and E - an immediate time saving.

After the divergent votes shown in Figure 14.4, we would probably want to analyze in more detail the reasons for and against proposals A, B and C. We could therefore run an evaluating ideas and proposals' session as described in Chapter 13 and illustrated in Figure 13.2 (p.120) to define in more detail the advantages and disadvantages of proposals A, B and C.

After suitable discussion we could repeat the vote for these three short listed proposals and see if there is any change. An extra round of focused discussion will often reduce the spread of the voting, and move the meeting towards agreement.

Thus Electronic Voting avoids the situation after the conventional vote of Figure 14.2 that five people leave the meeting in complete frustration, since their worst proposal has actually been selected as the best - and the chairperson innocently believes that there is consensus in the team to drive the project forward!

It is of course possible that the votes will stay divided even after all proposals have been fully discussed. Perhaps the Quality people are convinced that something must be done and the Finance people know there is no money to do it. The meeting can clarify this disagreement and close in a constructive fashion. We have a complete statement of the position of each side, and can pass the decision onwards or upwards.

It could happen that the five people in support of proposal A were the people with responsibility for it, and the people voting against it were at the meeting because of some other item on the agenda. The easy safeguard against this situation is that only the appropriate people vote on any issue.

In different situations, different voting techniques would be used. If there are limited resources to allocate, participants could vote by allocating the scarce resource (for example money, time or floor space) across the list of projects.

When there is a long list of items to deal with a *multiple-choice* vote is ideal. Each participant selects perhaps 10 items from a list of 50 or 30 items from a list of 150. There is no priority between these items as selected by the participants, but when the results of the vote are displayed in a histogram, similar to Figure 14.3, there are usually some clear favourites and some clear losers. This enables the list to be reduced; the shorter list can then be treated with more precision.

Care should be taken when using multiple choice voting that an idea is not present in the list several times with slightly different wording. If this happens the votes for the idea could be split over the several versions, each of which might get a low vote and be discarded. One solution to this is to merge similar items together before voting.

Other useful voting methods include four or five point scales, for example from 'strongly agree 'to strongly disagree, and a simple yes/no vote.

Matrix voting

The Electronic Voting described in the preceding example is vastly superior to the voting arrangements available in conventional meetings. Matrix Voting is even better yet. As applied in Electronic Meetings Matrix Voting is a revolutionary tool for analysis and decision making. It allows participants to explore and discuss reasons for a decision in a manner never achieved before.

A matrix is a table of data, similar to a spreadsheet. As the name implies, Matrix Voting sets up a matrix for votes to be entered. The proposals to be prioritized are in the horizontal rows of the matrix and the criteria for prioritization in the vertical columns.

To illustrate the process, let us use it to assess with yet more precision our five proposals A, B, C, D and E. We start by asking the meeting owner or the participants to define the criteria for making a choice between these proposals. This can be a very challenging question. The participants to the decision are of course aware that risk, payback, customer satisfaction, technology leadership, effect on the environment, investment required, etc. should somehow be included in their judgment, but they have not previously defined these criteria since they have not had an effective tool for handling them.

In this example we will consider four criteria and again use a scale of 1 - 10:

* speed of payback of investment
* effect on the environment
* effect on customer satisfaction
* degree of risk.

The proposals need to be important to justify this depth of analysis - Matrix Voting can be time consuming and should not be applied to minor issues. The participants rate each proposal against each criterion. Figure 14.5 illustrates the input window for the five proposals, with the entries partially completed.

Figure 14.5 - Matrix Vote input window

Matrix Vote input window				
	Payback	Environment	Cust. Sat.	Risk
Proposal A	8	9	5	2
Proposal B	6	6	8	9
Proposal C	3			
Proposal D	7			
Proposal E	2			

The results would be shown as a bar chart similar to Figure 14.3 where the horizontal axis shows the numeric total of the votes. In absolute terms the totals have little meaning, what is being achieved is a consistent comparison of the proposals.

We would perhaps hope to find a clear winner from this vote, but more often might find that two or three of the proposals justify further discussion before final selection. We could consider several approaches:

1. As in any vote we could have a further electronic discussion on detailed advantages and disadvantages of the remaining proposals (as in Figure 13.2 in Chapter 13) and we could then revote.
2. We could put weightings on those criteria that are of more importance. For example, the meeting might consider that 'effect on customer satisfaction' is twice as important as the other criteria. The results could be instantly recalculated on this basis. The proposals that score highly in 'effect on customer satisfaction' would move up the list in relation to the others.
3. We could analyze the voting for the three best proposals – focussing on the votes with a high spread or deviation. We might for example find significant disagreement between participants' votes on 'effect on customer satisfaction' for Proposal C, So the meeting can discuss and revote on this one proposal for this one criterion.

This capability of Matrix Voting to focus discussion with such precision on the key issues is quite exceptional. In this case we could focus on one criterion for one proposal out of four criteria for five proposals.

As with all votes, the details of the Matrix Vote can be kept and used to consistently explain the decision to anyone who was not present at the meeting. Equally the record can be deleted if so decided.

Taking responsibility for actions

Assigning individual responsibility for actions is an integral part of many meetings. In some circumstances of course it is entirely appropriate that the meeting owner does this but if the participants are to be involved, there are many ways of doing it in Electronic Meetings, including for example, a variation of Matrix Voting. The list of tasks is put into the rows of the matrix and the people, teams or departments are put into the columns. This is illustrated in Figure 14.6

Figure 14.6 Allocation of tasks to teams using Matrix Voting

Allocation of Tasks				
Task	Team 1	Team 2	Team 3	Team 4
Contact key prospects	0	0	1	0
Develope brochures	0	0	0	1
Arrange demos	0	1	0	0
Plan Electronic Meetings	1	0	0	0
Contracts and pricing	0	0	1	0

The participants vote by entering a 1 in the appropriate position of the matrix. Other fields remain at zero. The voting spread is then analyzed and discussion focused on any disagreements. This is a highly productive way of achieving agreement.

Another approach to assigning names and dates to tasks is to display the list of tasks to participants as though asking for their comments. Participants can add their comments; claiming responsibility for tasks or if appropriate allocating them to others. This is a simple electronic conversation, with the usual advantage that everything is on the record for access at any time in the future.

Summary

Voting in an Electronic Meeting is vastly superior to voting in a conventional meeting. Electronic Voting identifies where there is divergence of opinion, focuses discussion on the key issues and records the important points.

The voting techniques of Electronic Meetings are so powerful that it is surprising that important decisions can still be made only on the basis of a primitive show of hands.

Electronic Meetings are a very effective tool for taking and allocating responsibility for actions.

Electronic Voting is eminently suitable for distributed meetings, i.e. participants do not need to be in the same room to give their votes.

We have seen in the last four chapters the basic sessions that can go into Electronic Meetings. There are as many variations of these basic sessions as there are types of meetings, and they can be run in any sequence and changed instantly as required.

So now its time to get down to some of the practical issues in running Electronic Meeting.

MAKING IT HAPPEN

Chapter 15

RUNNING ELECTRONIC MEETINGS

So now we have covered the basics:

- two chapters of introduction
- eight chapters with a wide variety of business applications
- four chapters of detail about how Electronic Meetings actually work.

This next chapter describes some of the key points in getting maximum value from Electronic Meetings. The chapter is addressed to the meeting owner, i.e. the person who will be chairing the meeting, and is responsible for the outcome.

Figure 15.1 outlines the main steps involved in planning and running Electronic Meeting. A more detailed checklist of activities is given in the Appendix.

Figure 15.1 - Outline steps for an Electronic Meeting

• specify the *objectives* and *deliverables* of the meeting
• plan the agenda with a facilitator
• choose the participants
• ensure all practical meeting arrangements are made
• run the meeting with the facilitator
• ensure appropriate follow-up actions take place
• arrange your next Electronic Meeting

In this chapter we assume that the meeting owner has had no training or significant experience in Electronic Meetings so is working with an experienced facilitator who helps plan and run the meeting.

Planning an Electronic Meeting

Subject of the meeting
Be sure that you are tackling an issue or issues that are important to you and to the meeting participants.

Working with a facilitator
The facilitator should be some one with whom you feel confident to share responsibility for the success of the meeting. He or she should organize all aspects related to computing - you should not need to be at all concerned with computers unless you wish to be.

The facilitator will work with you to plan the meeting and develop the agenda. This should be an interesting analytical exercise and the time will be fully justified in terms of a well-run meeting and high quality deliverables. You may find it of value to (re)read Chapters 11 - 14 regarding the different types of sessions that can constitute an Electronic Meeting.

Specifying the deliverables
The most important single issue in planning an Electronic Meeting is to specify clearly what *deliverables* you require from the meeting. By *deliverables* we mean a physical output that can be printed or e-mailed. *Deliverables* might include, for example, a list of ideas, a detailed discussion of a set of topics, voting results, a set of recommendations or an agreed plan of action. Chapter 11 has a discussion about deliverables and objectives.

Set high expectations when you decide what you want out of the meeting – in an Electronic Meeting you should be able to discuss more deeply, get more ideas, develop the action plan further, get real commitment and/or actions in place more quickly than in a conventional meeting.

The participants

The participants should be all the key people involved in the subject of the meeting, or their suitably authorized representatives. In an Electronic Meeting you should expect to make real progress - and you do not want to do this with some key players missing or some participants not properly briefed. The participants do not need any training before the meeting.

Detailing the electronic agenda

Your initial ideas for the meeting may change as you and the facilitator develop the steps to achieving your deliverables. Between one and two hours is a reasonable estimate for planning a half day or a one day Electronic Meeting. Be aware that short meetings sometimes require more careful planning than longer meetings because there will be less time to react if the plan does not quite work out.

When planning for the meeting you will need to consider what input you want from the participants. One approach for an input session is to give participants a clear structure for their ideas and/or comments ('here is a set of proposals, please enter what you see as the advantages and disadvantages under the following headings'). The input - and probably the meeting - will be easier to manage, but the tight structure may restrict original and lateral thinking. Another approach is to ask for unstructured input ('please put all your ideas in, everything that might be relevant'). There is likely to be some duplication with this approach and some time may be needed to organize the input into a useful structure. However, by giving participants more freedom you may get a more complete picture and your participants may feel more involved in the results of the meeting. Ideas on how to structure participants' input were discussed in Chapters 11 - 13.

When collecting ideas or comments, you need to take a view on whether the session should continue until every last idea or comment has been squeezed out of the participants, or whether to limit the time for input and encourage the participants to make their most important points first. In the latter case, it is good practice to warn the participants at the beginning of the session rather than to suddenly cut them off in mid sentence when you decide that you have enough input.

The maxim '*vote early/vote often*' helps construct more effective Electronic Meetings. In the few minutes needed for an electronic vote it is possible to get an accurate view of the participants' opinions. This avoids wasted discussion on issues where there is already substantial agreement, and ensures that time is spent on the issues that really matter to you and the participants.

After a first discussion with you the facilitator should be able to draw up the electronic agenda. This agenda will lay out the flow of the meeting, with tools to be used and estimated timing, plus the parameters for each session (e.g. participants to see each others input or not, anonymous or not). The facilitator and you may need a short follow-up discussion to go through the detail of this agenda.

Measuring meeting effectiveness

It is important that in some way you measure the effectiveness of your Electronic Meetings, and the measures of success should be defined in advance. Participant feedback is valuable as one measure of success, for example whether participants felt that they had been able to make the points that they wanted, and whether they felt the important issues had been fully discussed.

However, participant satisfaction can be overvalued as a measure of a meeting. The bottom line value of a meeting lies in producing effective business output and does not necessarily correlate with a high level of participant satisfaction.

During the meeting

The facilitator should give participants a brief introduction to Electronic Meetings if appropriate. This introduction should include the strategic potential of Electronic Meetings, to give participants a long-term interest in the subject.

You can be pragmatic about keeping the meeting to the timetable. It is good to show occasional flexibility, so that the participants feel in control of the agenda, and not the other way round. It is technically very easy for the facilitator to modify the agenda of an Electronic Meeting in flight.

The interplay between you and the facilitator during the meeting can be expected to work out in a relaxed and easy fashion, with the facilitator being responsible for dealing with the technology, such as starting and stopping the computer sessions and explaining vote analyses.

As in a conventional meeting, the chairperson frequently needs to arbitrate on subject issues and on matters of timing and sequence. You should also be prepared to challenge participants if you are not happy with the depth of discussion or quality of ideas. The facilitator can perhaps do this, but may not have sufficient knowledge of the subject to know if difficulties are being glossed over or issues neglected. Either you or the facilitator should point out if, as sometimes happens, participants in their enthusiasm are entering ideals and comments that are ambiguous or otherwise unclear.

When an anonymous electronic vote is taken, it is important to make its purpose clear to the participants in advance, so that they are comfortable when you take a decision on the basis of it. For example, if you announce a vote as being a quick 'see where we stand' vote, then try to avoid the temptation of grasping it as the participants' final word on the subject if it just happens to turn out the way you want it.

During many Electronic Meetings there are periods of verbal discussion that need to be summarized for the electronic record. You might ask one of the participants to do this or sometimes the facilitator types in a few sentences under the watchful eye of the entire meeting.

Try to build into the meeting an atmosphere of creativity and fun, particularly if some of the participants are at their first Electronic Meeting. Inexperienced participants tend to dive into the technology with the fierce concentration of computer games addicts (including most of the people who protest that they can't type and don't like computers). Hence a little lightening up of the meeting can be appreciated.

Occasionally comments entered under the cover of anonymity are not appropriate to a serious meeting. These can easily be publicly deleted after the laughter has died down.

In general the seriousness, helpfulness and honesty of opinions expressed in Electronic Meetings contribute to an experience that participants find very worth while and are very keen to repeat.

Remote participants

You may have remote participants, linked to the meeting by their PC and a good quality telephone connection. These participants can share the discussion and enter their own ideas as if they were in the room. If this is their first Electronic Meeting the remote participants will need an introduction to the technology in advance. Remote participation is not as comfortable as being present at the meeting, so the remote participants should be very clear about the business reasons for the meeting and why they cannot attend in person. They are likely to need some extra time and attention from you and/or the facilitator to ensure that they do not feel isolated.

End of meeting survey

As described in Chapter 11, it is always good practice to have an on-line survey at the end of an Electronic Meeting to find out what the participants thought about the meeting and to collect their ideas to improve future meetings. Share this feedback with the participants before they leave the meeting.

Follow up

The electronic record of the meeting may need some tidying up if it is to be understood fully by people who did not attend the meeting. This could involve putting some of the intermediate discussion into appendices or adding some explanation to put discussions in context.

Please be prepared to spend some time in follow-up activities after the meeting. There is likely to be plenty of output if this is a first Electronic Meeting because participants will be unburdening themselves of ideas, suggestions and comments that they may not have previously expressed.

Hopefully one of the follow up activities will be to plan future Electronic Meetings, widening the number of people involved. Using Electronic Meetings across the whole organization is the subject of the next chapter.

Chapter 16

IMPLEMENTING
ACROSS THE ORGANIZATION

By developing solutions cost-effectively and creatively, Electronic Meetings offer vital benefits to all organizations. However, Electronic Meetings represent a significant change and as with any change, there is risk as well as opportunity. Machiavelli wrote to this effect (in 1513, before the development of Electronic Meetings):

"..there is no more delicate matter to take in hand, nor more dangerous to conduct, nor more doubtful in its success, than to set up as a leader in the introduction of changes. For he who innovates will have for his enemies all those who are well off under the existing order of things and only lukewarm supporters in those who might be better off under the new."

Nevertheless, changes in organization and culture as a result of the introduction of new computer technologies are now commonplace. Word processors, computerized stock control, CAD, electronic mail, and the Internet are well known examples of technologies that were first met with suspicion but are now a familiar part of the scenery.

The first introduction of Electronic Meetings can be risk free - and low cost - by hiring a facilitator and equipment from outside the organization. A small number of trial Electronic Meetings produce immediate benefits, as well as giving people experience of the technique and confidence in its value.

However, studies of technological innovation show that initial success does not guarantee that a technology will spread easily across the organization. Significant management involvement may be required to convert the initial heady enthusiasm into a day to day business tool. During the process of assimilation the technology may be 'reinvented' as different people take ownership of it or adapt it to their specific requirements. Eventually the new technology will become institutionalized in major business processes and fully accepted.

So how do we make this one fly? A set of outline steps would be:

> set up trial Electronic Meetings
> establish the business case
> order and install equipment
> select and train facilitator(s)
> demand measurable and visible results
> monitor on-going performance

Let us first look what effect Electronic Meetings are likely to have on the organization.

The effect on the organization

Meetings will be

> better planned
> more open and honest
> larger (if appropriate)
> run with some or all participants in different locations
> more creative

Solutions will be implemented more quickly because:

* meetings can be arranged sooner

- important issues will surface and be dealt with immediately
- meetings will be more decisive because all the relevant people can participate
- peoples' commitment at the end of meetings will be clear
- records of meetings will be available instantly
- there will be no delay for multiple smaller meetings.

A new management ethos will develop for meetings, in the same way that many other activities have become speedier and more precise using computers. Meetings will only be arranged when really needed and when they have clear objectives.

The feasibility of larger meetings does not imply that there is no place for small Electronic Meetings. The features of Electronic Meetings are equally valuable to meetings with as few as three or four participants. Small meetings still need structure and the benefits of instant documentation.

Some organizations already have rooms permanently set up for Electronic Meetings. People reserve these rooms as required, making contact with a facilitator if they wish.

Once people have attended face-to-face Electronic Meetings, different time/different place distributed meetings will follow naturally. Thus any group of people, whether they are on the same site or in remote locations, will be able to link into a quickly organized Electronic Meeting and conclude the issue there and then.

Of course not all meetings held in the organization will be electronic. But people who have experienced Electronic Meetings will no longer accept badly run conventional meetings, so all meetings will improve.

And just to repeat, Electronic Meetings do not mean that every decision is taken by a committee. Effective and useful Electronic

Meeting can be held to summarize opinions or make recommendations to an individual decision-maker.

Meetings are vital to any organization so it is perhaps surprising that conventional meetings remain such an organizational 'black box', in the sense that it is never clear what happens inside them. Electronic Meetings on the contrary can be audited like any proper business process. Objectives and results can be monitored, as can participant satisfaction. Benchmarks can be carried out to ensure that Electronic Meetings are being used where they are most beneficial to the organization, consistent with best practice around the world.

In these days of fast decision making, extensive distributed working and increasingly 'open book' management, Electronic Meetings are the natural way to run the organization.

The business case for Electronic Meetings

To establish a business case for Electronic Meetings, an assessment of the costs and the benefits is required.

Costs will be involved in obtaining the computer hardware and software for Electronic Meetings and in training facilitators. Technical networking skills will be needed to set up and maintain the networks. Calculating the costs of such resources is a standard process. The real challenge is measuring the benefits.

This book has described many benefits of Electronic Meetings. To measure these benefits one can:

• estimate the direct cost savings from shorter meetings and lower travel costs
• survey participants on the value of better business outcomes
• access the scope for Electronic Meetings in the organization.

- consider some of the organizations who are using Electronic Meetings

Direct cost savings

Results of Electronic Meetings using GroupSystems software have been measured at IBM and Boeing. Ron Grohowski of IBM recorded more than **60% person-hour savings over 30 projects**. "Furthermore administrative costs fell; calendar time was reduced and the number of meetings required to complete a project diminished".

At Boeing, Brad Post reported on 64 Electronic Meetings involving a total of 654 participants. The savings are extremely impressive, as shown in Figure 16.1.

Figure 16.1 - Savings from Electronic Meetings at Boeing

Savings to company:
$432,260 total labor dollars saved
$6,754 labor dollars saved per session
11,678 total labor hours saved (71%)
1,773 total days of flowtime saving (91%)

These figures justify repetition:

Labor hours reduced by **71%** and flowtime by **91%.**

The US Army Research found that "in a single session we were probably saving conservatively about $50,000 of travel and living expenses and $75,000 - $100,000 on personnel." This was on the basis that they were able to get "4 - 6 weeks work done in three and a half days."

Evidence of time and travel savings from distributed meetings has also been reported. For example, Jenny Flowers and Beth

Nave of Bellcore estimated 60 to 70% timesaving using Electronic Meetings to facilitate their performance management process. In addition, by running distributed Electronic Meetings, Bell saved $10,000 for each meeting!

David Brown at the US Department of Fish has reported saving upwards of $1,000 per participant per day when running distributed Electronic Meetings (i.e. same time, different place meetings), based on the time and costs of travel. This rate of cost saving pays back an investment of approximately $75,000 relatively quickly!

Better business results

As well as direct cost savings, the objective of Electronic Meetings is to reach better solutions. This is difficult to measure, but one approach is to ask the people who attended the Electronic Meetings for their opinion.

Figure 16.2 - Feedback after Electronic Meetings at Boeing

Question	Average Response
A decision by consensus was reached	4.77
Organization has made use of output/product	4.83
TeamFocus has improved decision making and information gathering	5.04
Required results were obtained from the session	4.88
TeamFocus allowed organization to shorten schedule or reduce resource usage	5.04
Facilitator and services added value	5.54
Would use TeamFocus again	5.38

By sending out a follow-up questionnaire several weeks afterwards, Brad Post measured whether people believe that they take better decisions in Electronic Meetings. Twenty-four people responded, on a scale of 1 - 6. The feedback is shown in Figure 16.2 (TeamFocus was an IBM name for its Electronic Meeting service).

It can be seen that, on a scale out of 6, participants reported agreement above 5 that Electronic Meetings:

- improved decision making,
- shortened schedules
- reduced resource usage.

Figure 16.3 - Feedback from Electronic Meetings at NationsBank
(Shermer and Daniel)

NationsBank Group	Number of participants	Mean Usefulness Rating
NationsBank/Vendor Planning	10	9.4
Control GroupSystems Planning	63 (multiple sessions)	7.62
Private Bank Reengineering	15	8.15
Legal Counsel Systems Requirements	5	9.00
Strategic Technology Planning	25	7.00
Product Initiatives Development	9	7.60
Standards & Contract Redesign	8	8.60
Strategic Issues	5	8.80
Communications Planning Session 1	10	8.40
Communications Planning Session 2	18	8.1
Marketing Olympic Loans	12	8.30
Marketing-Olympic Themes	10	7.9
Ideal Environment-Requirements	12	8.92
Tech. Strategic Planning	14	8.07
Contracts & Standards	7	7.43
Info. Roadmaps Requirements Planning	14	9.07
Executive Info. Needs	11	8.64
Real Estate Information Needs	8	6.75
Premier Vision Project	7	9.29
Systems Planning	10	6.80
Car Loan Planning	9	7.78

Another assessment of the value of Electronic Meetings is provided by NationsBank. Suzie Shermer and Lynn Daniel have summarized participant evaluation as shown in Figure 16.3. The usefulness of the meetings is rated with an average above 8 out of 10 by nearly 300 participants, on a scale of 1 to 10. These are impressive numbers.-

The ability to collect such feedback is of itself a strong reason for using Electronic Meetings, since it might be well argued that all serious organizations should have a mechanism for measuring the effectiveness of a process as important as meetings.

Scope of Electronic Meetings

As well as extremely positive participant reaction, Figure 16.3 also illustrates the many different types of meetings run at NationsBank. The scope of Electronic Meetings is further illustrated by Bob Briggs and colleagues at the University of Arizona working with the U.S. Navy. The U.S.S. CORONADO is a command ship, a floating military command center awaiting the arrival of temporary Flag and General staffs in response to a crisis. These staffs work under high pressure and rely heavily on teamwork to achieve their goals. They often need the immediate cooperation of people who are distributed across the fleet and around the globe. Among the projects tackled with the help of Electronic Meetings were:

- achieving consensus in allocating a $10M budget in under three hours
- 75 officers preparing a unified budget submission in two days
- 30 senior officers and civilians redrafting in two days a constitution of the office of Chief Information (CIO) for the Navy. This was in response to a law passed by Congress.

- Simulating disaster relief operations live at three important Navy professional conventions, communicating directly with the First Marine Expeditionary Force and three ships.
- Six participants linking the U.S.S. CORONADO to experts at the Navy and Marine Corps War Colleges and a Marine Corps War Fighting Lab. The CORONADO took a simulated hit during this exercise, as a consequence of which the entire distributed Electronic Meeting was conducted without any voice or visual contact.
- 50 experimenters, who had been involved in 23 different technology experiments were debriefed in small groups for an hour each. A 75 page preliminary report was produced within a day, including recommendations for future directions.
- Eight officers participating in two brainstorming sessions to generate possible Courses of Action (COAs) by a simulated enemy that was massing troops on a border. Specifically the officers had to determine the enemy's most likely, least likely and most dangerous COA. 56 COAs were generated in 7 minutes, categorized in 6 minutes and prioritized in another 10 minutes. "They were ready to report to the commander in under half an hour, a task that might have taken three times that long by other means."
- Crew members inputting anonymous comments about the quality of life aboard the ship. These comments were categorized and sent unfiltered up the chain of command.

Who uses Electronic Meetings?

The names of organizations using Electronic Meetings have been referenced throughout the book, a small proportion of the organizations that might have been quoted. No one should now feel that in using Electronic Meetings they are venturing into the unknown!

Another organization that has recorded its successful use of Electronic Meetings is JP Morgan, a global supplier of financial services to corporations, governments, financial institutions and other large organizations. JP Morgan established a Decision Support Center (a permanent Electronic Meeting room) in New York in 1991. By June 1994 JP Morgan had opened two more centers (in Delaware and in London) and had conducted over 1000 Electronic Meetings in major financial centers around the world.

KPMG's Electronic Meeting center in Holland is called the Ervarium. Stephanie Ottenheijm has recorded that over 200 meetings were run in its first year of operation, many of them on strategy development work for clients.

PricewaterhouseCoopers are one of the largest commercial users. They use Electronic Meetings in client workshops internationally to support their audit services. These workshops address risk management issues and the needs of corporate governance in all industry sectors. There can be few organizations that would not benefit from using Electronic Meetings for this purpose.

Selecting and training facilitators

Formal training for people who are going to facilitate Electronic Meetings is essential. A two-day course is sufficient for facilitators to be able plan and run their first meetings provided they have appropriate personal backgrounds of business experience and receive some initial support. Facilitators should match their growing skills with the type of meetings they facilitate and ensure that they keep up-to-date with current practice in what is a very fast moving field.

Many Electronic Meetings are easy to run, for example when the meeting is relatively small, the subject is familiar and the participants are supportive. Such meetings do not need a facilitator once the chairperson and participants have acquired some experience in Electronic Meetings. However, if the meeting is large, the agenda is full, the participants are senior or the subject is very political, a facilitator is likely to add value.

Some organizations prefer to use external facilitators for particularly confidential or challenging meetings.

Setting demanding targets

It is important to set demanding targets for Electronic Meetings and to check that the required results are achieved. If there are unsuccessful meetings, the reasons should be analyzed and used as a basis for learning for future meetings.

To get optimum results, information about this new technique must be communicated in a structured manner. People who are not yet involved with Electronic Meetings need to understand what is happening. People and project managers should be informed about the potential benefits, perhaps by giving them a copy of this book - a low cost, effective means of communicating the scope and basic techniques of Electronic Meetings.

Resistance to Electronic Meetings

Even when the business case is established, there may still be resistance to Electronic Meetings from people who do not want changes to organization's culture, from those who fear that their influence might be reduced, and also from those who are still afraid of using computers. A number of objections against Electronic Meetings have been thrown up over the years and it may help the reader anticipate them by listing some of them here:

- it is unnatural to plan meetings
- we don't need anonymity, everyone is open and honest
- if Electronic Meetings were that good we would already be using them
- we don't need participation, I already know what my people think
- I can't take the time to evaluate all those ideas produced by Electronic Meetings
- I need to know who says what so I can do annual performance reviews
- why would I want to involve other people in decisions?

Hopefully this type of objection will be overcome by patient example and by encouraging people to participate in Electronic Meetings.

The decision to use Electronic Meetings across the organization should be based on what is being achieved today, but it will also involve consideration of what the future offers. This is the subject of the next, and final, chapter.

Chapter 17

THE FUTURE FOR
ELECTRONIC MEETINGS

In one sense the future of Electronic Meetings is not a major issue for this book, which is about the present and what is available **now**.

Nevertheless when assessing the likely benefits from Electronic Meetings we want to be sure that the system will be strategically well placed in the light of probable developments in:

• computing technology
• social trends
• business requirements

Developments in computing technology

The most conspicuous trends in computing are falling prices and increasing power. Current laboratory developments are such that we can expect these trends to continue for at least the next fifteen to twenty years. Cheaper laptop computers, larger display screens, wireless networks, longer lasting batteries and faster networks will make it continuously easier and more convenient to hold Electronic Meetings anywhere, anytime.

With cheaper computing technology, voice channels and video-conferencing will more fully integrate into the base technology that supports Electronic Meetings. The Internet will presumably continue to offer low cost networking technology to the world and all the benefits of electronic business.

Electronic Meeting software is usually positioned within the range of computing tools known as *Groupware*. Groupware can be seen to have three levels as illustrated in Figure 17.1. Electronic Meetings sit appropriately at the top level.

Figure 17.1 - Three levels of Groupware

3. **Decision and action**	- group and team work - **Electronic Meetings**
2. **Co-ordination**	- keeping the group in touch - electronic mail - shared data bases - electronic conferencing
1. **Individual**	- making people productive - spreadsheets - word processors

Electronic mail and other computer-based techniques at the co-ordination level are immensely useful in the preparation of Electronic Meetings and in the speedy distribution of the deliverables where appropriate. But these co-ordination tools do not substitute for meetings, where people contribute personal judgment, creativity and enthusiasm in addition to the knowledge that can be stored in computer databases.

Social trends

Electronic Meetings are thoroughly consistent with the major current trends in organization, including flatter hierarchies, distance working and reliance on teamwork.

Furthermore, Electronic Meetings can clearly help satisfy the increasing expectations of more open organizations and decision making. Many organizations are accountable to a public that is demanding much more information than the annual financial report. For a whole range of issues, including risk management and anything related to the environment, organizations are expected to show that decisions were taken on a sound basis with all reasonable speed.

Another conspicuous social trend is the use of computers in schools and universities, leading today's students to access the Internet for information as naturally as their parents opened books. To people with this mindset using computers in meetings will be natural and sensible. Not to use computers in meetings will become the exception.

Changes in business requirements

Most organizations are undergoing continual pressure for change, and there is no reason to expect that this pressure will decrease in the next few years. This need for change reinforces the value of Electronic Meetings. The Electronic Meeting solutions described in this book are in business areas that will remain vital to all organizations, including:

- Responding to customers
- Strategic planning
- Business Process Re-Engineering
- Supplier Management
- Risk management
- Quality
- Human Resources
- Skills management
- Education and Training
- IT.

Hence in key areas where there is particular pressure to perform with excellence and at the same time to change, Electronic Meetings have been specifically shown to be successful in achieving results.

Summary:

The Electronic Meetings described in this book are in the key business areas and strategies of the future. Social trends support the business case for Electronic Meetings. Developments in computing technology will continue to make Electronic Meetings cheaper and easier to run.

Electronic Meetings will immediately benefit all organizations and will remain in the strategic front line for the foreseeable future.

Appendix

Check list for an Electronic Meeting

> This appendix contains a suggested checklist of questions as guidance for setting up an Electronic Meeting.
> The meeting owner and the facilitator will usually consider these questions together.

Planned date and duration of the meeting:
Subject of meeting:
What significant business objective does this meeting support?
What does the meeting contribute to this business objective?
Deliverables of the meeting:

    1.

    2.

    3.

Who will chair the meeting?
Who will facilitate the meeting?
What are the measures of success of the meeting:
- for the meeting owner?
- for the participants?
- for any others who might have a view?

Type of Electronic Meeting:
- face-to-face
- distributed, i.e. face-to-face with some remote participants
- different time/different place

When will the agenda be finalised?

When will the list of participants be agreed?
Who has confirmed that the participants are the right people to
    achieve the objectives of the meeting?
Who will inform the meeting participants about the meeting?
Who else needs to be informed about this meeting?
Participants' level of experience with Electronic Meetings?
        None   Low   Medium   High
What information is to be circulated in advance of the meeting?
What information is to be available at the start of the meeting?
Who else should be told that the meeting will take place?
Who is responsible for equipment and facilities:
- meeting room layout
- network of PC's
- overhead projector
- copying facilities
- refreshments and lunch.
Who will open the meeting?
Does the agenda of the meeting include:
- timing and instructions for each session
- a survey of participants' satisfaction with the meeting?
Who will distribute the documentation from the meeting?
Who is responsible for follow up actions from the meeting?
Any other issues which might affect the success of the meeting?

References

Adkins, M., Shearer, R., Nunamaker, J.F. Romero, J., Simcox, F. Experiences using Group Support Systems to Improve Strategic Planning in the Air Force. *31st Annual Hawaii International Conference on System Sciences,* 1998.

Arsenault, D., Using a twenty station portable with two hundred participants, *Seventh Annual GroupSystems Users' Conference*, 1996.

Asch, S.E., *Effects of group pressure upon the modification and distortion of judgements,* in H. Guetzkow (ed.), Groups, Leadership and Men. Pittsburg, PA: Carnegie Press 1951.

Bongers, F.J., Strategy Development, Participatory Scenario Workshops and GroupSystems, *GroupSystems Worldwide Conference*, 1998.

Boshes, M., Group User Feedback Techniques for Product Development, *Seventh Annual GroupSystems Users Conference*, 1996.

Briggs, R., Mittleman, D., Directed Brainstorming: Techniques that Improve Idea Generation *GroupSystems Worldwide Conference*, 1998.

Briggs, R., Mittleman, D., Weinstein, N., Nunamaker, J.F., Adkins, M., Collaborative Technology for the Sea-Based War Fighter: A Field Study of GSS Adoption and Diffusion, *31st Annual Hawaii International Conference on System Sciences,* 1998.

Buckingham, P., Livernois, L. and Frazier, P., Consolidation of Government Information systems in the Department of Defense, Seven*th Annual GroupSystems Users' Conference*, 1996.

Campos, R.M. and Macias, A.L.T., Strategic Planning Process: Mexican Government and Industry Application, *GroupSystems Worldwide Conference, 1998*.

Cesserani, J. and Greatwood, P. Innovation and Creativity, Kogan Page, London, 1995.

Chenault Group, Benchmarking Best Practices with Focus Groups in Healthcare, *Fifth Annual GroupSystems Users' Conference*, 1994.

Corbitt, G. and Wright, L. Enhancing Business Process Redesign: Using Tools to Condense the Process, *Thirtieth Annual Hawaii International Conference on System Sciences,* 1997.

Cukierman, C.L., The Master Clinical Lexicon: Integrated Product Team Approach, *31st Annual Hawaii International Conference on System Sciences,* 1998.

Daniel, L., Using GroupSystems V in Product Design, *Fifth Annual GroupSystems Users' Conference*, 1994.

Davison, R.M. and Briggs, R. O., GSS for presentation-style meetings, *Thirtieth Hawaii International Conference on System Sciences,* 1997.

De Bono, E. *Six Thinking Hats,* Penguin Books, London, 1986.

De Vreede, G., Support for Collaborative Design: Animated Electronic Meetings, *Thirtieth Hawaii International Conference on System Sciences,* 1997.

Dean, D.L., Lee, J.D. and Nunamaker, J.F., Group Tools and Methods to Support Data Model Development, Standardization and Review, *Thirtieth Hawaii International Conference on System Sciences,* 1997.

Fisher, R. and Ury, W. *Getting to Yes, negotiating agreement without giving in*, Penguin Books, New York and London, 1991.

Flament, C. and Rose, N., Using GroupSystems V to facilitate painful decisions: a downsizing saga, *Sixth Annual GroupSystems Users' Conference*, 1995.

Flowers, J. and Nave, B., GroupSystems – A Quality Team Integrator, *Fifth Annual GroupSystems Users' Conference*, 1994.

Gardner, M., Techniques for extending GroupSystems, *Seventh Annual GroupSystems Users' Conference*, 1996.

Gieszl, L. and Speigel, R.F., GroupSystems for Warfare Analysis, *Fifth Annual GroupSystems Users' Conference*, 1994.

Glynn, M.S., Quintana, J., Cunningham, D. and Cooper, S., GSS For Jury Deliberations: Applying Technology in the School Courtroom, *31st Hawaii International Conference on System Sciences,* 1998.

Griffen, D.S., Integrating GroupSystems with Strategy and Leadership Development, *GroupSystems Worldwide Conference, 1998.*

Grohowski, R., Mcgoff, C., Vogel, D., Martz, B., Nunamaker, J., (1990) Implementing Electronic Meeting Systems at IBM: Lessons learned and success factors', *MIS Quarterly, University of Arizona*, 1990.

Herniter, B.C., Carmel, E. and Nunamaker Jr, J.F., Computers improve the efficiency of the negotiating process, *Personnel Journal,* April 1993.

Holt, J.R., Assessing the Efficacy of Information Technology Systems at Academic Medical Institutions, *31st Hawaii International Conference on System Sciences,* 1998.

Huber, M.W. and Dennis, A.R., Mum's not the Word! An Investigation of the Effects of a Group Support System on a Men's Counseling Group, *31st Hawaii Conference on System Sciences,* 1998.

Janis, I. *Psychological studies of policy decision*, 2nd edition, 1972.

Jones, A.N. and Miller, D.E., Using Technology for Stakeholder Consultation, The World Bank's Use of GroupSystems V in Developing Countries, *Thirtieth Hawaii International Conference on System Sciences,* 1997.

Kelly, K., The Global Workplace: Using GroupSystems for Intercultural Awareness, *GroupSystems Worldwide Conference*, 1998.

Lagumdzija, Z., Mission Impossible: GroupSystems in Sarajevo 1995, *Seventh Annual GroupSystems Users' Conference*, 1996.

Lewis, L.F. and Shakun, M.F., Using a Group Support System to Implement Evolutionary System Design, *Group Decision and Negotiation,* 5:319-337, 1996.

Lindsay, C.B., GroupSystems Goes Public: Redefining Meetings for Local Government, *Seventh Annual GroupSystems Users' Conference*, 1996.

Lindsay, C.B. and Thomas-Campbell, N., Duets: Harmonizing GroupSystems with other software, *GroupSystems Worldwide Conference*, 1998.

Lockhart, E., Using GroupSystems in Strategy and Team Development, *Sixth Annual GroupSystems Users' Conference*, 1995.

Lonsdale, M., GroupSystems in the Classroom: Using Technology to support Group Thinking, *GroupSystems Worldwide Conference*, 1998.

168   ELECTRONIC MEETINGS

Lowry, T., Rinehart, D. and Hoffman, D., How Do We Get There, Planning your Process, Integrating Technology and Achieving your Goals, *Sixth Annual GroupSystems Users' Conference*, 1995.

Lynch, M.P. and Wood, W.K., Using Electronic Meeting Systems for Subject and Course evaluation, *Thirtieth Hawaii International Conference on System Sciences,* 1997.

Middendorf, K., Product Satisfaction Workshop, *Fifth Annual GroupSystems Users' Conference*, 1994.

Moore, G. and Piety, E.N., How to stay organized during a revolution, Six*th Annual GroupSystems Users' Conference*, 1995.

Neal, R.L. and Cole, M.A., Building a Virtual Partnership: The Federal Emergency Management Agency's Experience with Distributed Group Collaboration, *GroupSystems Worldwide Conference, 1998.*

Nicol, L., Steering Corporate Development with Consumer Views, *Sixth Annual GroupSystems Users' Conference*, 1995.

Nunamaker, Jr, J.F., Dennis, A.R., Valacich, J.S. and Vogel, D.R. Information Technology for negotiating groups: generating options for mutual gain, *Management Science, Vol 17, No. 10*, October 1991.

O'Brien, B. and Renner, A., Improving Faculty Input, Research Collaboration and Classroom Instruction using GroupSystems, *GroupSystems Worldwide Conference,* 1998.

O'Donnell, L. Conducting Focus Groups in the Groupware environment, *Fifth Annual GroupSystems Users' Conference*, 1994.

Ottenheijm, S., van Genuchten, M. and Geurts, J., What's the Problem? How Groups can develop a shared conception of a Problem using an Electronic Meeting System, *31st Hawaii International Conference on System Sciences,* 1998.

Petrun, C.J., Using GroupSystems V to Facilitate the Change Management Efforts of the US Government, *Sixth Annual GroupSystems Users' Conference*, 1995.

Phillips, D. and Basha, C., Implementation of GroupSystems in Diversified Cultures, *GroupSystems Worldwide Conference,* 1998.

Post, B.Q. (1992) 0073-11299-1/92, IEEE.

Rizzi, J. A., Reengineering the Vendor Selection Process, *Fifth Annual GroupSystems Users' Conference*, 1994.

Røyksund, C., Heltne, M.M. and Wee, L.C., Managing Change Collaboratively in a Liberal Arts College, *GroupSystems Worldwide Conference,* 1998.

Shafer, E. and Csonka, M., Streamlining the Failure Mode and Effects Analysis, *Seventh Annual GroupSystems Users' Conference*, 1996.

Shermer, S. and Daniel, L., GroupSystems at NationsBank: Adding a Technological Edge, *Seventh Annual GroupSystems Conference*, 1996.

Shortt, D., GroupSystems and Strategic Planning, *Seventh Annual GroupSystems Users' Conference*, 1996.

Svaneborg, E., Andersen, V. and Mora-Jensen, C., Streamlined Supply Chain Management by way of GroupSystems Remote Surveys, *GroupSystems World Conference 1998.*

Teti, F.M., Workforce Diversity - Assessment, Feedback and Planning using GroupSystems Tools and Processes, *Seventh Annual GroupSystems Users' Conference*, 1996.

Tyran, C.K., Dennis, A.R., Vogel, D.R. and Nunamaker, J.F., Jr., The Application of Electronic Meeting Environment to Support Strategic Management. *MIS Quarterly*, September 1992, pp 313-334.

Van Genuchten, M., Cornelissen, W. and van Dijk, C., Supporting Inspections with an Electronic Meeting System, *Thirtieth Hawaii International Conference on System Sciences,* 1997.

Wilkerson, G., Bridging Manual Project Planning with Categorizer and Group Outliner, *Fifth Annual GroupSystems Users' Conference*, 1994.

Details of some of these references and further information on Electronic Meetings in general can be found on the publisher's web site: www.emsl.co.uk.

Index